Printed in the United States of America

Table of Contents

Spirituality, Change and Motivation

Assessment, Clinical Evaluation, Treatment Planning, Family and Community Education and Case Management

Professional Responsibility and Ethics

Practice Examination -

Introduction

Congratulations on selecting a career as a Credentialed Alcoholism and Substance Abuse Counselor. You are undertaking difficult, rewarding and necessary work, but you will make a difference in the lives of the people whom you help to treat every day.

Here is a brief overview of the resources you will find in this study guide:

- An explanation of the structure of the CASAC exam
- A description of the topic areas covered in the exam
- Exam scoring information
- Review of the exam format: multiple choice questions, case history, etc.
- Basic CASAC exam rules
- How to prepare for the exam
- Understanding multiple choice testing
- Types of memory skills needed to answer questions
- Studying for the exam
- Scheduling study time
- Antidote for procrastination
- Productive study skills
- Before the exam: 2 weeks, 1 week, 1 day, day of exam
- Taking the exam
- Mental attitude
- Stress management, pacing, reducing fatigue
- Pros and cons of changing answers
- A detailed review of answering multiple choice questions
- Sample exam questions
- A simulated 60 minute exam

The certification examination will test you in eight domains. The learning objectives of each are listed here:

Domain 1: Clinical Evaluation

- Demonstrate effective verbal and non-verbal communication to establish rapport.

- Discuss with the client the rationale, purpose, and procedures associated with the screening and assessment process to facilitate client understanding and cooperation.

- Assess the client's current situation, including signs and symptoms of intoxication and withdrawal, by evaluating observed behavior and other available information to determine client's immediate needs.

- Administer the appropriate screening and assessment instruments specific to the client's age, developmental level, culture, and gender in order to obtain objective data to assess client's current problems and needs.

- Obtain relevant history and related information from the client and other pertinent sources in order to establish eligibility and appropriateness to facilitate the assessment process.

- Screen and assess for physical, medical, and co-occurring disorders that might require additional assessment and referral.

- Interpret results of data in order to integrate all available information, formulate diagnostic impressions, and determine appropriate action.

- Develop a written summary of the results of the assessment in order to document and support the diagnostic impressions and treatment recommendations.

Domain 2: Treatment Planning

- Discuss diagnostic assessment and recommendations with the client and concerned others to initiate an individualized treatment plan that incorporates client's strengths, needs, abilities, and preferences.

- Formulate and prioritize mutually agreed-upon problems, immediate and long-term goals, measurable objectives, and treatment methods based upon assessment findings for facilitating a course of treatment.

- Use ongoing assessment and collaboration with the client to review and modify the treatment plan to address treatment needs.

Domain 3: Referral

- Identify client needs that cannot be met in the current treatment setting.
- Match client needs with community resources appropriate to their abilities, gender, sexual orientation, developmental level, culture, ethnicity, age, and health status to remove barriers and facilitate positive client outcomes.
- Identify needs differentiating between self-referral and counselor referral.
- Explain to the client the rationale for the referral to facilitate the client's participation with community resources.
- Continually evaluate referral sources to determine effectiveness and outcome of the referral.

Domain 4: Service Coordination

- Identify and maintain information about current community resources in order to meet identified client needs.
- Communicate with community resources concerning relevant client information to meet the identified needs of the client.
- Advocate for the client in areas of identified needs to facilitate continuity of care.
- Evaluate the effectiveness of case management activities through collaboration with the client, treatment team members, and community resources to ensure quality service coordination.
- Consult with the client, family, and concerned others to make appropriate changes to the treatment plan ensuring progress toward treatment goals.
- Prepare accurate and concise screening, intake, and assessment documents.

Domain 5: Counseling

- Develop a therapeutic relationship with clients, families, and concerned others in order to facilitate self-exploration, disclosure, and problem solving.
- Educate the client regarding the structure, expectations, and limitations of the counseling process.
- Utilize individual and group counseling strategies and modalities to match the

interventions with the client's level of readiness.

- Continually evaluate the client's level of risk regarding personal safety and relapse potential in order to anticipate and respond to crisis situations.

- Apply selected counseling strategies in order to enhance treatment effectiveness and facilitate progress towards completion of treatment objectives.

- Adapt counseling strategies to match the client's needs including abilities, gender, sexual orientation, developmental level, culture, ethnicity, age, and health status.

- Evaluate the effectiveness of counseling strategies based on the client's progress in order to determine the need to modify treatment strategies and treatment objectives.

- Develop an effective continuum of recovery plan with the client in order to strengthen ongoing recovery outside of primary treatment.

- Assist families and concerned others in understanding substance use and utilizing strategies that sustain recovery and maintain healthy relationships.

- Document counseling activity to record all relevant aspects of treatment.

Domain 6: Client, Family, and Community Education

- Provide culturally relevant formal and informal education that raises awareness of substance use, prevention, and recovery.

- Provide education on issues of cultural identity, ethnic background, age, sexual orientation, and gender in prevention, treatment, and recovery.

- Provide education on health and high-risk behaviors associated with substance use, including transmission and prevention of HIV/AIDS, tuberculosis, sexually transmitted infections, hepatitis, and other infectious diseases.

- Provide education on life skills, including but not limited to, stress management, relaxation, communication, assertiveness, and refusal skills.

- Provide education on the biological, medical, and physical aspects of substance use to develop an understanding of the effects of chemical substances on the body.

- Provide education on the emotional, cognitive, and behavioral aspects of substance use to develop an understanding of the psychological aspects of substance use, abuse, and addiction.

- Provide education on the sociological and environmental effect of substance use to develop an understanding of the impact of substance use on the affected family systems.
- Provide education on the continuum of care and resources available to develop an understanding of prevention, intervention, treatment, and recovery.

Domain 7: Documentation

- Protect client's rights to privacy and confidentiality according to best practices in preparation and handling of records, especially regarding the communication of client information with third parties.
- Obtain written consent to release information from the client and/or legal guardian, according to best practices and administrative rules, to exchange relevant client information with other service providers.
- Document treatment and continuing care plans that are consistent with best practices and applicable administrative rules.
- Document client's progress in relation to treatment goals and objectives.
- Prepare accurate and concise reports and records including recommendations, referrals, case consultations, legal reports, family sessions, and discharge summaries.
- Document all relevant aspects of case management activities to assure continuity of care.

Domain 8: Professional and Ethical Responsibilities

- Adhere to established professional codes of ethics and standards of practice in order to promote the best interests of the client and the profession.
- Adhere to jurisdictionally-specific rules and regulations regarding best practices in substance use disorder treatment in order to protect and promote client rights.
- Recognize individual differences of the counselor and the client by gaining knowledge about personality, cultures, lifestyles, gender, sexual orientation,

special needs, and other factors influencing client behavior to provide services that are sensitive to the uniqueness of the individual.

- Continue professional development through education, self-evaluation, clinical supervision, and consultation in order to maintain competence and enhance professional effectiveness.

- Identify and evaluate client issues that are outside of the counselor's scope of practice and refer to other professionals as indicated.

- Advocate for populations affected by substance use and addiction by initiating and maintaining effective relations with professionals, government entities, and communities to promote availability of quality services.

- Apply current counseling and psychoactive substance use research literature to improve client care and enhance professional growth.

Knowledge of Alcohol and Substance Abuse
(85 Hours)

Key Concepts in Addiction and Alcoholism

There are several key concepts involved in addiction and alcoholism. While the use of alcohol and drugs is normal behavior for some, addiction to these substances occurs when there are behavioral, cultural, and physiological elements present. Two people using the same substance can have a completely different reaction to the substance, and addiction is present when the individual is impaired due to use of the substance.

Consequences of Impairment

Impairment causes:

- Inability to keep a job or attend school.
- Use of substances in high risk situations, such as while driving.
- Legal consequences due to use of drugs.
- Encountering conflicts due to alcohol or substance use.

The Psychology of Addiction

According to researchers, the concept of addiction is highly influenced by the psychological state of the patient. Further research is being conducted in order to determine if the patient experiences addiction due to a mental health issue, or if the addiction is actually a disease. Addiction to drugs presents itself psychologically, in a manner that is similar to other forms of addiction, such as gambling.

The psychological factor explains why patients who have an addiction often jump from one drug to another. The psychology behind addiction suggests that the high of the drug is not something that is sought after due to its mind-altering effects, but rather due to the pleasure that is received by getting the drug of choice. The physical addiction that occurs over time is not due to the psychological factor.

Methods of Assessing Addiction

The psychological state of a person can be used as a factor when assessing addiction. By using factors based upon the person's addiction status and their current emotional status in life, the chance of recovery increases. The elements of addiction assessment include:

- *Patient reports* - Getting reports from the patient on when they are active or non-active in addiction.
- *Using empathy* - This is done when discussing the substance abuse test results with the patient who receives treatment.
- *Biomarkers* - Lab testing is not considered reliable, and should not be used solely to measure a patient's progress. Instead, biomarkers should be used to evaluate the patient's progress.

Purpose of Biomarkers

Biomarkers will allow you to track a patient's recovery process and identify risks of addiction based upon their previous psychological patterns and behaviors. Biomarkers can be detected in both urine and blood tests. These can be used to detect if the patient is using on occasion or if heavy use is present.

Psychological Elements of Addiction

Understanding the unique psychological aspect of a patient's addiction is important to successful recovery. Without understanding this aspect of addiction, recovery is difficult to maintain as these emotions continue to rise. The psychological aspect of a person's mind frame can affect the process of addiction. There are three different elements contained within the psychological aspect of addiction.

- *Sense of powerlessness* - Addiction is often accompanied by feelings of helplessness and powerlessness. The feeling is often experienced after the use of the substance.

- *Sense of hopelessness* - A sense of overwhelming hopelessness.

- *Sense of rage* - Rage is a feeling that people experience when they suffer emotional injury, and when this feeling occurs in those who abuse substances, it is known to be the fuel for substance abuse. The rage may cause the person to show irrational, destructive behavioral patterns. The way that rage is expressed in an individual plays a large role in addiction. For some, their rage may allow them to take action that will help them. For those who have a substance abuse problem, the rage is turned inwards, and instead of directing that rage positively towards the cause, substance use takes place.

The Pharmacology of Alcohol and Other Drugs

Each substance has a specific effect on the body and mind. The addiction factor for each substance is compared when treating a patient with addiction. The species, gender, method of administration, and strength of the drug all determine the level of addiction present.

Important Pharmacology Terms

- *Drug:* An illegal substance used to create a high within the body.

- *Medicine:* A drug prescribed to a patient to treat a condition. It may have a potential for abuse, and if this is present, the use should be monitored.

- *Misuse:* Using a drug in a manner, or for a reason that differs from how it was prescribed. This type of use is unintentional.

- *Abuse:* Using a drug in a manner other than prescribed, with the intention of getting high, such as taking too much.

- *Dependence:* A state that occurs when drug or alcohol abuse has persisted for a prolonged time. The person can become both mentally and physically addicted to the drug.

- *Psychological dependence*: When a person has a strong mental urge to use a drug to experience the effects considered to be pleasant (drug or alcohol used to reach a euphoric state of mind)

- *Physical dependence*: Occurs when a person's body is used to taking the drug, and they start to experience withdrawal symptoms when the drug is no longer present in their system.

- *Cross-dependence*: A person may use another drug form to lessen the withdrawal they are experiencing from their drug of choice.

- *Tolerance:* The body will adjust to a drug over a prolonged time, and the effects will not be the same when taken. Tolerance often leads to taking larger amounts of the substance to try to achieve the same effects.

- *Reverse tolerance*: This can cause a person to become more sensitive to the drug over a period of time, rather than less sensitive. It will cause the substance to have a higher level of impact on the person when taken.

- *Dose:* How much taken at one time or over the course of 24 hours.

- *Half-life*: The amount of time the drug stays present within the body. This level can be affected based upon metabolism and other factors, which differ from the specific half-life of the drug.

- *Lethal dose*: When the dose of a drug taken is too potent and results in death.

- *Therapeutic dose*: The amount of drug needed in order to be effective.

- *Drug interactions*: The way that drugs interact with one another. This includes interactions between street drugs, prescription drugs, and alcohol.

The way the drug is administered can affect its method of action. For example, a drug may be stronger when taken intravenously, when compared to the oral administration method. There are different forms of administration for each substance. Abuse of a substance can occur when the method that is traditionally used for the drug is altered. For example, a drug is turned into liquid form and inserted in the body through a syringe, rather than taken orally as prescribed.

Oral Administration

The most common method of drug administration is the oral route, where the drug comes in pill or capsule form. Some medications that are taken orally have restrictions that make it necessary for the medication to be taken orally. For example, a time-released medication will need to be taken by mouth and cannot be crushed, or the time release action will be disrupted, and too much of the medication can be provided to the person during one period of time. Other methods of administration are generally used when the medication is not available in pill form, when the patient needs a faster acting medication, or if the patient is unable to swallow the medication while in the pill or liquid form .

Inhalation

Certain drugs can be taken through inhalation methods, but this is very seldom used as a prescribed form of administration. While the use of marijuana is approved in some states for certain conditions, the patient that you are working with will be able to provide you with clear documentation of the prescription if this is the case.

Intranasal (Snorting)

Intranasal drug use is also called snorting. This is commonly used among those who abuse oral medications, as this method of administration allows the drug to enter the bloodstream much quicker than when it is taken orally. While the effects are fast acting, the side-effects can be very dangerous, and in some cases, deadly. Those who use this method of administration can cause severe damage within the sinus cavity, and brain damage can also occur with both short and prolonged usage.

Suppositories

While not all drugs can be taken rectally, certain drugs such as cocaine can be taken through a suppository. The mucus membranes in the rectum area can absorb some drugs quickly. This can be risky because you cannot predict the sensitivity level of the membranes, and the drug can be absorbed much faster, or to a greater extent than with other forms of administration.

Intravenous (I.V.) Administration

The use of drugs through a syringe is common among those who use a variety of different substances. With injection, the drugs are supplied directly into the bloodstream, and the effects occur immediately.

Some drug users will use the drug in different areas of the body by intramuscular or subcutaneous injection method, as veins and muscles can become damaged with prolonged injections applied to the same areas. These include:

- Intramuscular injections inject the drug right into the muscle.

- Subcutaneous injections inject the drug into the soft tissue under the skin.

When drugs are taken through injections, there are additional risks present. While the risk of overdose is high with this method of administration, the risk of contracting a disease is also increased. This is because if a needle is shared with someone who has a disease, it can be easily spread to the next person. The risk of an infection is also high when using this method, as many drugs require the use of cotton, which can get stuck within the syringe and get under the skin. Infections can also occur due to lack of proper preparation, which creates an unsterile environment.

Eating/Drinking

Administration is also done orally by eating or drinking a substance. Drinking is common with alcohol, but certain drugs need to be eaten in order for them to work properly, such as LSD or "magic" mushrooms containing psilocybin.

Toxicology Testing

There are different testing methods that collect information on the type, amount and last use of a drug. There are three common toxicology testing methods used which include: urine, blood, and saliva testing methods. In rare cases, the sweat or the contents of the stomach can be used. However, these are rarely used in toxicology testing involved with addiction.

Urine Testing

With urine testing, a urine sample is collected within a sterilized container, and the container may already have the testing device on it. If the test needs additional screening, it can be sent to a laboratory, which will provide more accurate testing results. This includes the amount of the drug present in the urine, which can indicate the amount and the last time the drug was used. Urine testing must be done within five days of the collected sample, as the drug begins to leave the urine at this time and an accurate test cannot be conducted.

Saliva Testing

With saliva testing, a swab made from cotton material is used to take a sample from the mouth. The mucus membranes within the mouth will have traces of the drug, which will then move into the saliva. This testing is done by using the swab on the inside of the cheek, and then enclosing the swab in a sterilized container that will be sent to a lab for testing.

Blood Testing

To perform blood testing, a blood sample is taken from the patient with a syringe. This method of testing is one of the most effective for drugs, as drugs can be detected in the blood much faster than urine and saliva, and they also stay in the blood for longer periods of time. One blood sample is all that is needed, regardless of the amount of drugs being assessed.

Drug testing in any of these forms can be done to check for one specific drug, or to check for up to 30 drugs at one time. The drug testing method used depends upon why it is being done. For example, if the test is taken for legal purposes, the examiner will look for a variety of drugs. However, when being used to help with addiction, one specific drug or those in a similar class are the focus.

There are many models of addiction treatment. The perspective of the client and his or her family will often indicate which approach will benefit the addict for the long term. There are numerous types of addictions, from drugs to gambling, from interpersonal relationships to sex. As many different types of addictions exist, there also are many models and theories of addiction. To be a successful model, the addiction model must blend multidimensional aspects of addiction with various cultural and regional aspects, interpersonal preferences, and family concepts.

Understanding Addiction Models and Theories

To understand models and theories of addiction, the counselor should:

- Have a complete understanding of the models and theories surrounding addiction, and how these affect the patient's addiction and recovery process.

- Develop an understanding of the appropriate models used to treat addiction.

- Master all terms related to theories and concepts involved in addiction.

- Develop an understanding of the proper methods used to evaluate addiction.

- Gain knowledge and understanding of all areas involved within the addiction process, which include the models of psychology, sociology, biology, genetics, and other dispositions.

- Understand the social, economic, and cultural aspects of addiction

- Evaluate each person's addiction status based upon their social, economic, and cultural stance.

- Understand all of the risk factors involved with addiction.

- Use statistical information gained from research.

Medical Model

The medical model of addiction is one of the most used because it is well established with most rehabilitation centers. In addition, it is a descriptive model that does not lead to one method of intervention. The outline of this model and the addiction process involves:

- *Genetic predisposition* - The person has a biological "addiction drive" and this explains why similar behavior leads to addiction in certain people.

- *Response to addictive chemicals* - The person has a specialized response to substances, which explains why taking a drug is not pleasant for some people, but others enjoy it.

- *Risk factors* - The model adopts the context issues of social environment, preexisting mood disorders, drug availability, and life issues.

- *Practice* - This involves a trial and error process by means of experimentation or "learning" how to use the drug.

- *Change from use to addiction* - This is when the brain changes from occasional use to full-blown addiction, which involves hyposensitation and hedonic dysregulation (the inability to feel good without the drug).

The broad nature of the medical model of addiction allows it to show each stage as a target for intervention. In addition, with this model, the responsibility of the addiction rests on the addict, even though there is a genetic predisposition to use drugs. The advantages of this model include generality, the ability for counselors and medical professionals to use their own judgment in each specific case, and that it disallows addictions that do not involve chemical substances.

Cultural Belief Model

The cultural beliefs of a patient must be addressed when providing patient care. For example, some people within different cultures may express emotional stress with physical terms. They may explain symptoms of depression as a headache, stomachache, or similar physical illness, while the effects are actually mental. Certain behaviors may be attributed to the culture of the patient, and it would be unethical to disrupt any behaviors that are related to culture. Certain expressions can also vary, and all of these different cultural aspects must be considered when first accessing the patient's drug addiction, and then again when creating an effective treatment method for the patient.

Moral Model

The moral model of addiction involves temptation, which is seen as the root of the addiction. This model also emphasizes spiritual aspects of recovery, also. Society tends to treat addiction as a character flaw, considering it a moral failing or medical condition that absolves the addict of his or her responsibility for the behavior.

The moral model has fallen out of favor with some rehabilitation centers because the medical community identifies addiction as a real disease process with a true genetic component. This is a dilemma for addicts, because they do not understand this process, and feel as if poor choices are the result of moral failings.

Causal Factors

1. Spiritual Deficit

2. Conscious Choice

Suggested Courses of Treatment

1. Clergy Intervention (Spiritual Guidance)

2. Moral Persuasion

3. Imprisonment/Social Consequences

Treatment Specialists

1. Clergy

2. Law Enforcement

Cognitive Model

The cognitive model of addiction is different from other model approaches to addiction. It moves away from biological, social, and emotional causes and focuses on cognition. Cognition is a mental process that relates to judgment, perception, and reasoning. With this model of addiction, counselors must find out what core beliefs allow the addict to engage in drug using behavior, both conscious and unconscious. There is no one-size-fits-all approach with this model. The cognitive model of addiction became popular in 2005, and combines addiction treatment with behavioral therapy. This combination attacks false beliefs and teaches the addict skills to deal with stress in a positive manner. Cognitive-based therapies are well-respected in the psychology environment, so this model is often used.

Bio-Psycho-Social Model

The bio-psycho-social (BPS) model of addiction is an attempt to explain how addiction starts, continues, and is maintained. This framework is an understanding that allows counselors to set up a treatment program. The biological factors of the BPS model involve genetics and chemical changes that occur from drug use, and are viewed as the primary cause for the addiction. The BPS model expands to include emotional (psychological) and social aspects of addiction. This model involves family matters, poverty, crime, opportunity, mental disorders, and the influence of friends. Critics of this model feel that it is too broad and does not really give a target to treat and attack. Practical addiction treatment tends to blend the BPS model with the medical model. Along with medications, treatment is often more successful.

Temperance Model

The temperance model is often confused with the moral approach. This model gained popularity during the 19th century with the prohibition movement. The core assumption of this model is that addictive and destructive power of a drug or substance is strong and the drug itself is the actual problem.

Psychological or Characterological Model

The characterological (psychological) model views the chemical dependency as something rooted in abnormalities of the addict's personality and character. Counselors who use this model say that the person has an "addictive personality" which is connected to the degree of personal and psychological boundaries. Traits that appear to contribute to this type of personality are low self-esteem, poor impulse control, inability to cope with stress, egocentricity, manipulative tendencies, and a desire for power and control.

Causal Factors

1. Personality or disposition ("addictive personality")
2. Low Self-Esteem
3. Poor Impulse Control

Suggested Courses of Treatment

1. Psychotherapy
2. Identification and modification of self-esteem, interpersonal skills, impulse control, improved boundary setting

Treatment Specialists

1. Psychotherapists
2. Social Workers with training in advanced practice

Social Education Model

The social education model is an integrative approach with principles from the school of classical and operant conditioning. The addiction is seen as a learned behavior, one that stems from modeling influences and cognitive processes. Counselors who use this model feel it is a cohesive philosophy recognizing precursory causes and further reinforcement of the behavior through operant conditioning. The addict is influenced by socialization processes, imitation of observable behavior, and role models.

Causal Factors

1. Poor Socialization
2. Poor Modeling
3. Poor Coping Mechanisms and Skill Deficits

Suggested Courses of Treatment

1. Correct estimation and realistic goal setting
2. Appropriate Modeling
3. Cognitive Exercises and Reconditioning
4. Skill Training
5. Impulse-Control Training

Treatment Specialists

1. Appropriate peer modeling
2. Cognitive / Behavioral counseling

The Biological Model

The biological model of addiction is based upon genetic factors that influence addiction. Genetics, biochemistry, and metabolism all play a role in biological addiction factors. Similar to the reaction that some people have to certain foods, some people may be unable to tolerate alcohol, even when consumed in small amounts. Their bodies will act adversely to the substance, and behavioral issues will occur. Women tend to have a lower tolerance to alcohol then men. When addiction occurs based on genetic factors, signs of addiction often show before the substance is used. Signs are seen at a young age, which include violent behaviors, impulsive behaviors, and deficient social skills. The enzyme MYOB may be lower in the brain of those who are susceptible to alcohol abuse due to their genetic disposition.

Genetics Theory

The genetic theory of addiction is also called addictive inheritance theory. This theory separates genetic and environmental factors of addictive behavior. Many research studies show that environmental components contribute to addiction, but numerous studies regarding alcoholism show that children born from alcoholic parents who are adopted by non-alcoholic families have a three to four times greater risk for alcoholism over the general population. Certain people are more at risk for addictive inheritance for substance use. Eskimos, Asians, and Native Americans are genetically predisposed to a deficiency in the production of acetaldehyde, the enzyme that degrades alcohol. This group is hypersensitive to the effects of alcohol. Also, all studies show that sons (rather than daughters) are more at risk to inherit alcoholism.

Exposure Theory

Exposure Theory is based on the assumption that being introduced to a chemical substance or alcohol on a regular basis will eventually lead to addiction. This implies that the body causes metabolic adjustments that require continued and increased doses of a drug in order to avoid withdrawal. If this is true, the drug mimics endorphins (natural pain killers or "feel good" chemicals) on a regular basis, and this will reduce the body's natural endorphin production, causing reliance and addiction.

Conditioning Theory

The basis of conditioning theory is that addiction occurs from the reinforcement of drug administration. With this theory, the substance acts as a potent reinforcer and gains control over the behavior of the user. Those who abuse a drug receive a highly rewarding effect, and the addiction is defined as a behavior refined by the pleasure.

Adaption Theory

The adaption theory involves psychological, environmental, and social factors that all influence the addiction process. Expectations and beliefs about the drug influence the user's behavior and reward him or her for the use of the drug. This theory recognizes that many factors (internal and external cues) contribute to the potential for addiction, along with many subjective emotional experiences. Research on this theory has focused on the psychodynamics of drug reliance, and studies have implicated causes such as ego deficiencies, child-rearing deficits, and other psychological issue.

There are two main concepts involved in the health and healing of addiction. The first process involves those who experience addiction alone, and the other involves those who experience addiction along with mental health disorders.

Mental Health Concept

Issues involving a patient's mental health are used as part of a treatment program when addiction is present. As research on the topic has expanded, awareness of providing patients with the proper treatment while at a mental health facility has included the use of addiction recovery methods. According to research studies, people with severe mental illnesses only experience success with recovery one-half of the time.

Concept of Recovery in Addiction

The concept of recovery in addiction is a plan that works by implementing a treatment program that provides transformational change in those who are going through the process of recovery. As knowledge continues to expand, the methods used to treat addiction also expand and various techniques used together can provide recovery to patients who are undergoing a treatment program. The methods used continue to expand as knowledge advances, and the idea behind this concept is to use a treatment plan that provides the patient with long-term positive effects.

The addiction advocacy movement was created in order to provide recovery to patients by involving their families. When connection with families is used as part of a treatment program, long-term recovery is achievable, as this allows the patients to receive support from their family members while undergoing the process of recovery from addiction. The concept of addiction is applied by reviewing the patient's current recovery process, and using new patient recovery plans when appropriate. The concept also implies that a shift in the recovery process must be used whenever it becomes ineffective for the patient.

The process of recovering from addiction requires the mental health aspect of the patient to be taken into consideration. This is true even if the mental health issues are present due to the addiction itself and are not caused by genetic factors. By addressing the mental health aspect of addiction, any issues present with the mental health status of the patient are evaluated prior to starting the recovery process. By treating the patient's mental health, the chance of a successful recovery increases. Therapy helps the patient gain the skills needed for long-term recovery.

Healing from addiction is a personalized process that occurs while the patient is going through the recovery process. As recovery advances, the personalized experience expands, and the patient becomes more aware of their unique recovery process, and the steps that need to be taken in order to keep their recovery on track. Each person undergoing the recovery process is responsible for his/her own recovery, and the tools provided by the consoler or group should be used to apply self-help tools on their own time while going through the recovery process.

The concept of recovery had first only taken into account the aspects involved in complete recovery. However, knowledge based upon partial recovery, and the concepts involved in this process have grown. Full recovery and partial recovery treatment options are now used in conjunction for those in recovery, and this combination of the two concepts has increased the promise of higher success rates.

Prevention

Prevention groups are defined as a group of individuals who are working together in order to provide education on drug use to a target group. The groups included in the process of intervention include: the general population, at-risk individuals, and high-risk individuals. The main goal is to stop drug use from occurring, but also to address the issue of abuse if it should occur by catching it while in the early stages. When the use of drugs has advanced, preventative measures should be taken in order to prevent further progression. The measures used should also be aimed towards restoring health in those who have just started use of drugs, and those who are advanced in use by providing education on drug resistance, decision making skills, and conflict resolution.

Preventive Methods

- Reducing the available supply of drugs and alcohol through appropriate measures, including legal assistance.

- Reducing the amount of demand present for drugs and alcohol by providing those in the community with appropriate treatment methods.

- Continuing development of treatment centers to improve level of care.

Primary Prevention

Primary prevention is used for young people or those with little to no history of drug/alcohol abuse. It is applied by:

- Promoting abstinence from drugs and alcohol.

- Teaching refusal skills to those who haven't used.

- Increasing "usage" policies, such as age limit to buy alcohol.

- Providing education on the dangers associated with drugs and alcohol use.

- Promoting safe alternatives by offering community activities to the younger generation.

Secondary Prevention

Secondary prevention is used to help addicts once early usage is detected by way of the HALT Theory. This includes:

- Use intervention method to stop drug/substance use and abuse.

- Provide education on the risks, dangers, and other negative factors.

- Provide skill-building techniques to help client refrain from further use.

Tertiary Prevention

Tertiary prevention is used when drug or alcohol use and abuse has become progressive, and promotes healing of the mind and body. This includes:

- Apply intervention processes to stop drug use and encourage recovery.

- Send the patient to appropriate detox facility to stop use safely.

- Use treatment center after detox to help ensure proper recovery process.

- Use a specialized approach to treatment that includes desensitizing users to triggers, such as people, places, things, and actions.

- Use pharmaceutical approaches to help recovery success.

- Create solid aftercare program for treatment after the initial program is complete.

- Teach the 12 step principles to the patient in order to prepare him or her for aftercare.

Intervention

Intervention is a process in which a group of people work together in order to interrupt addiction. This offers recovering addicts several options that can be used to stop the process of addiction. Also, intervention can prevent the individual from hitting rock bottom, and it works to reorient those who have lost touch with reality during the addiction process. The intervention process involves meeting with the family and significant others of the addict, who will be assisted through the process with the help of a counselor. The process is successful when applied using the correct measures of detached caring.

Steps of Intervention

Several steps are involved in the process of intervention. These include:

- Gathering the intervention team together.

- Making lists of incidents and occurrences that are of concern regarding the addiction.

- Designating one individual to be the chairperson for the group, who is often the person closest to the addict or the counselor.

- Determining the reading order process that will be used during the intervention.

- Developing a list of firm, realistic steps that will be used by each team member during the intervention.

- Gathering information on available treatment options to present to the addict during the intervention process. The list must be created taking different factors into consideration, such as affordable treatment options and locations of open treatment centers.

- Deciding upon the date and time that the intervention will take place.

Benefits of Intervention

While an intervention is not always successful for the addict, the process can still be successful for those involved. This is because it offers different benefits which include:

- Coming together for the first time as a family since the addiction started.

- Learning techniques that family members can use for self-help.

- Stopping denial of the addiction in both family members and the addict.

- Learning as a group how to stop enabling addiction.

Treatment

The treatment process must be viewed as continuous. The treatment used for recovery is determined based upon certain criteria that the patient meets. To determine the level of addiction present and place the addict into the appropriate category, the counselor must decide which category applies. These include:

- *Non-user* - This person does not or has not used substances.

- *Moderate and non-problematic user* - This person uses some substances occasionally, but the use has not had a negative effect on the patient's life so far.

- *Heavy and non-problematic user* - This person uses substances heavily, but hasn't had negative effects occur with health or life.

- *Heavy with serious problems* - This person uses substances very often, and has had many negative events occur due to use.

- *Heavy with moderate problems* - This person uses often and has had a few issues occur as a result of the use.

- *Dependent and addicted with life and health problems* - This person is unable to stop drugs due to physical and mental addiction, and the use and abuse of substances has caused issues in the patients personal life, as well as had a negative effect on their health.

Steps for Treatment

Providing treatment for addiction requires the following steps in order for it to be effective:

1. *Identify:* Screen the areas of the patient's life affected by the addiction and identify the level of addiction present in the patient.

2. *Assessment:* Collect various pieces of information from the patient, and those involved in the patient's treatment plan, to identify the patient's strengths, weaknesses, and treatment goals. Use information gained during the assessment to create long-term treatment plan for the patient.

3. *Stabilize:* Stop addiction to the substances using appropriate methods. Some methods include; detox and use of pharmaceutical alternatives in order to help stop addiction and create a secure recovery foundation.

4. *Rehabilitate:* Determine the proper long-term treatment program for the patient based upon the issues detected during the assessment and development of overall treatment plan.

Types of Rehab Programs

Rehabilitation (rehab) programs are all designed to help the addict stop the process of addiction, but there are different forms of the program available. These include:

- *Co-occurring treatment centers:* These facilities offer treatment to patients who have mental health and substance abuse issues.

- *Inpatient facilities:* These units are designed to treat patients who stay at the facility over the entire course of treatment. Treatment generally lasts from one to six months.

- *Outpatient facilities:* These centers offer the same type of care as inpatient rehabilitation facilities, except the patient leaves the facility and goes home after the treatment is completed each day.

- *Aftercare program:* Typically used for patients that have successfully completed an inpatient or outpatient rehab program. These programs may be used for patients who experience addiction without life issues, and when it is determined that addiction may be stopped with a less aggressive treatment program.

Each of these programs work to initiate the initial recovery process. The initial process is vital, but there must also be further preventative measures used to stop relapse from occurring once the treatment program is complete. These preventative measures are offered to the patient during the time of treatment. They include:

- Identifying triggers that could lead to substance abuse again.

- Determining which coping methods can be used in order to stop a relapse when a trigger occurs.

- Addressing any personal issues related to the addiction in the patient.

- Helping the patient work through issues to help with recovery.

Goal Setting

An important part of any treatment program is to set goals with the patient. Goals are based upon the patient's desires, and are created using realistic measures. When goal setting is used, it offers several benefits which include:

- Makes the recovery more obtainable by creating steps to reach the goal.

- Reviews goals frequently in order to maintain recovery and stay on track.

- Shares success stories when goals are reached to maintain progress.

Drug Substitution with Alternative Pharmaceuticals

Some patients may benefit from replacement pharmaceuticals, which are designed to assist the patient in the first stages of recovery. When using a drug substitution, review the pharmaceutical used and be sure that the patient is using it properly. This will increase the chances of success at the treatment center and afterwards.

Addiction Therapy

Addiction therapy is offered during treatment in three different forms.

1. *Individual therapy:* Provided to patient on a one-on-one basis. This offers patients the ability to speak about personal issues, and learn coping techniques to help them work through barriers to a successful recovery.

2. *Group therapy:* Offers the patient the ability to participate in a group setting with peers who also face addiction. This gives the patient the opportunity to relate to others with similar issues, as well as to develop a support team.

3. *Family therapy:* Used to help the addict and family members work through issues that may have occurred during active use. This type of therapy also helps members of the family to understand the addiction process, as well as to obtain skills to assist the patient through the recovery by using supportive techniques and eliminating denial.

The 12 Steps

Step 1 - We admitted we were powerless over our addiction - that our lives had become unmanageable

Step 2 - Came to believe that a Power greater than ourselves could restore us to sanity

Step 3 - Made a decision to turn our will and our lives over to the care of God as we understood God

Step 4 - Made a searching and fearless moral inventory of ourselves

Step 5 - Admitted to God, to ourselves and to another human being the exact nature of our wrongs

Step 6 - Were entirely ready to have God remove all these defects of character

Step 7 - Humbly asked God to remove our shortcomings

Step 8 - Made a list of all persons we had harmed, and became willing to make amends to them all

Step 9 - Made direct amends to such people wherever possible, except when to do so would injure them or others

Step 10 - Continued to take personal inventory and when we were wrong promptly admitted it

Step 11 - Sought through prayer and meditation to improve our conscious contact with God as we understood God, praying only for knowledge of God's will for us and the power to carry that out

Step 12 - Having had a spiritual awakening as the result of these steps, we tried to carry this message to other addicts, and to practice these principles in all our affairs

A successful recovery is based upon the addict taking control of the recovery process and making it a personal goal. There are several programs used to help the patient develop self-help techniques, which increase the chances of a successful recovery. The main area of focus used within the various self-help groups is the 12 steps, which were created as the original principles for Alcoholics Anonymous. These steps are also used for other groups as a self-help recovery tool. The 12 principles all have an important step in the recovery process.

Common 12 Step Rehabilitation Programs

Various rehabilitation programs use these principles, but the steps have changed to fit the needs of the different programs. The 12 steps are used for both addicts and family members of addicts who are working as part of the recovery treatment process. Some of these programs include:

- *Alcoholics Anonymous (AA):* A fellowship of men and women who come together in order to share their experiences, strength and hope for recovery. The only requirement to join this is to have the desire to stop drinking.

- *Narcotics Anonymous (NA):* A non-profit organization meant for men and women who face major drug problems. The meetings are held in order to help maintain sobriety.

- *Al-Anon:* Fellowship for families who are not addicts, but who have one in their family. Members are trying to understand the addiction and how they can manage their own lives.

- *Al-Teen:* A fellowship for younger family members that works off the same principles as Al-Anon.

Additional Self-Help Groups

- *Rational Recovery:* This group of addicts supports each other through the use of rational recreation therapy. The therapy is based upon the use of rational thinking as the way to recovery.

- *Moderate Management:* This group is not for addictive drinkers. Rather, it is for non-addictive drinkers who face life issues as a result of their drinking patterns.

- *The Secular Organization of Sobriety:* This group uses the one-day-at-a-time method of thinking. Members of the group face addiction with both drugs and alcohol.

- *Women for Sobriety:* This is a spiritual-based group that uses the 12 steps, along with some AA principles. The main focus is to use positive emotion as the way to stay sober.

Knowledge of Addiction

The experiential practicum in knowledge of addiction requires that the proper knowledge is gained by the counselor who works with people experiencing drug addiction. In order to provide the patient with the right care, several areas must be examined during the initial intervention, treatment, and preventative processes used for the patient. The areas of addiction that must be addressed include:

- Identify the type of addiction that is present.

- Determine the level of readiness to change that the patient displays.

- Identify any problems and beliefs related to the addiction.

- Provide several levels of patient care to the patient, and individual, group, and family therapy should be used in conjunction when appropriate.

- Advocate for patient care.

- Take active participation in patient's treatment plan.

- Make referrals to appropriate professionals when needed for additional treatment.

- Keep an accurate record of patient care.

- Work as a team with others involved within the patient's treatment plan.

- Act as a positive role model for those receiving the care.

- Provide the patient and public with information on preventative measures that can be taken in order to help prevent addiction.

- Continue education process by keeping up with the most recent information provided regarding addiction, effective treatment, and other areas involving treating patients with addiction problems.

The skills acquired while working towards a degree must be applied to each case during the initial phases of treatment, as well as while going through the treatment process. Any changes made to the processes should be evaluated, and then applied to the patient's care program.

Prevention, Intervention, and Treatment

Upon completion of written and oral course work completed at the rehabilitation facility or program, 12 step students must apply the knowledge gained during their education in order to develop their skills through hands-on learning. For training as a student of the 12 steps, the following aspects must be completed:

- Provide self-help strategies to a person in the recovery process.

- Hold various self-help groups for those in recovery.

- Guide another addict through the steps involved with the 12 step principles.

- Upon completion of the group practice, the student must determine how effective their approach was, and decide what changes to make.

Sharing

During the 12 steps, and upon completion, the student must record their findings, which includes any questions that they may have. They will then share their findings with other group members. The steps allow the student to observe different practices used for self-help, which will allow them to examine the behaviors of the group, what seems to be effective, and experience applying self-help to those in recovery first hand.

Process

- Determine why the self-help counselors are an important part of the group.

- Determine which type of group is most effective for individuals based upon their history of use and various individual factors.

- Determine how the patient's census concepts are learned and applied.

Alcoholism and Substance Abuse Counseling
(150 Hours)

Universal Precautions

The treatment staff must apply the same precautions used by hospital staff when they are treating those infected with the human immunodeficiency virus (HIV) or acquired immunodeficiency syndrome (AIDS) virus. All addicts should be considered infected, whether test results confirm this or not. The universal guidelines fall under the national Institute of Occupational Safety and Health Administration (OSHA). Any contact with fluids needs prompt attention, as transmission occurs right away. The treatment provided to the staff includes antiviral therapy to stop the spread of the virus through the body. This should occur within the first few hours of contact.

HIV/AIDS

HIV is a contagious virus that can be spread via blood and body fluids. This is a growing epidemic among IV drug users. Studies show that the HIV has the fastest transmission rate among all other sexually transmitted diseases (STDs). It is most common among those who inject drugs. This virus can spread quickly among social groups in which multiple members engage in unprotected sex with each other.

The HIV virus lives within the cells of the body and dies once it is outside of the. When the virus meets oxygen, it will die right away. Transmission occurs through:

- *Intercourse* - During intercourse, HIV is transmitted between people through the mucous membranes found in the rectum and vagina.

- *Saliva exchange* - Transmission can occur through the transfer of saliva. While this is less likely, it is still a possibility.

- *Shared needle* - When infected blood is caught within a needle and injected directly into a non-infected user, this will almost always cause HIV. Blood is not the only fluid that transmits HIV, however; it can be spread when any body fluid goes from the incision back into the syringe chamber. Detecting this type of transmission is impossible with the naked eye, so drug users should never share syringes.

There is an increased risk for those with STDs in the form of lesions, cuts, and open sores. This means that those who have a prior STD are more likely to get HIV due to open lesions that could easily be subjected to the virus. The HIV virus can be transmitted from one person to another even if it is newly detected. For example, someone may have just been infected with HIV virus, are not be aware that they have the virus, and are able to transmit it to another person. Once the HIV virus is passed to another individual, it spreads rapidly. The virus begins within the area that it entered, typically the blood or sexual organs in drug use situations. It will then quickly spread through the blood and start attacking the body. This occurs when the virus is in progression, and transmission is greater when suppression of the immune system is present. Treatment can be provided for HIV in its earliest stages. While there is no cure for this type of disease, treatment in the early stages of the disease, can delay infection of the entire body. Once suppression of the immune system occurs, there is no way to treat the HIV virus and it will turn into AIDS, which is fatal.

Early Symptoms of HIV

- *Dark lesions* – These could occur anywhere on the body.
- *Changes in vision* – A change within a person's vision is often one of the early signs of the HIV or AIDS virus.
- *Unexplained fevers* – Usually worse at nighttime.
- *Headache*
- *Fatigue*
- *Swollen lymph glands*
- *Unexplained rash*

Sexual Issues and STDs

Sexual intercourse plays a role in the transmission of several STDs. Risky sexual activity is not just intercourse, but includes other activities, such as oral sex. Drug addicts often offer sex in exchange for drugs when addiction has progressed.

Prevention of STD Transmission
Stopping use with treatment lowers the risk of transmitting various STDs. This is done by reducing the amount of risky behavior in the patient. In order to reduce the risk, the patient must be provided with a treatment plan that is focused upon stopping addiction, rather than seizing transmission. While stopping both behaviors is

important, without an active addiction, the probability of contracting an STD is greatly reduced. The patient should also be educated on the exact way in which HIV transition occurs, as well as other STDs. Drug use, active substance abuse, STDs, and mental health issues are intertwined when it comes HIV transmissions. Often, if each factor is not addressed during the treatment process, it will cause another factor to react, and the process will start over again.

Risk Reduction Counseling

The process of risk reduction counseling involves using substance-abuse prevention in order to stop the spreading of STDs. This form of counseling offers information regarding changes of transmission when it comes to risky behaviors. During this time, any questions that the patient may have will be answered. The patient should also be provided with factual information regarding the transmission of AIDS or HIV during the early stages of these during the counseling session. This process of HIV education helps the patient to understand the importance of change, and how without change, he or she can encounter serious issues with health by getting this devastating illness. During this counseling session, the risk reduction counselor offers information on developing skills needed to change. For example, many patients lack a proper support group, which can result in use of drugs. If their peers use syringes during the process of using drugs, they will be more likely to use drugs with this method of administration. If they don't get the coping tools to stay away from their old situation or uses, relapse, advanced use, and the possibility of transmission will increase.

Education

To educate the recovering addict, the counselor should provide information on the risks associated with injection. This education will not only be provided to people who are in the early stages of recovery, but it should be provided to those are actively using. This process is done by encouraging cessation of substance use and the use of clean syringes. While it is not always possible for the addict to stop the substance use completely, by providing the patient with the proper education, he or she could reduce the risk of contracting HIV or another STD.

- *When the Addict is Actively Using:*
  - Provide proper coping skills.
  - Give information on ways to build the immune system.
  - Discuss the benefits of exercise.
  - Teach self-exams to detect issues regarding patient's health.

- *Offer External Resources to Patient*
  - Housesitting
  - Residential program
  - Home healthcare
  - Support groups
  - Info and treatment options that are available

The Counselor's Role

- Take proper precaution steps when working with a patient who has an STD, especially HIV or AIDS, but always treat them with the same care and respect as those who do not have an infectious disease.

- Provide support to the patient in order to help them cope with their disease. This is especially important for those just learning that they have the virus. Offer the patient educational information, such as pamphlets and brochures.

- Discuss different treatment options available for the patient regarding the disease. Treatment must be focused upon recovery, but can be used to discuss diseases. This is done in a way that will help the patient to feel hope for the future. When a patient feels hopeless, it can lead to relapse.

- Offer the patient the steps needed for behavioral changes. While the HIV virus cannot be eliminated, providing a patient with useful information needed for behavioral change will help prevent relapse. Additionally, this will reduce the likelihood of actively using again and the possibility of spreading the virus to other people who have drug addiction problems.

- Someone who has an incurable STD may be less likely to take behavioral change seriously, so provide the patient with information on the serious nature of the disease in order to offset the possibility that they may contact a worse condition in the future.

Preventing STD Infection

Case workers and alcoholism and substance abuse counselors must provide the patient with tentative methods of avoiding STD infection. These include:

- Proper education on different types of STDs, and how they affect a person's life, well-being, health and future.

- Instruction on the use of standard precautions as a part of everyday life. The patient may not be aware of which precautions they should take in order to reduce the risk of transition. Precautions make the patient less likely to encounter a STD and able to better protect themselves.

- Ensure that the treatment used is one that is aimed towards both recovery from drugs and alcohol and prevention of STDs.

- Take the steps needed to identify relapse within the patient and put a stop to it. By working with the patient, you'll be able to identify different trigger cues or behaviors that indicate when a relapse is going to occur.

Helping Patients Stay in Recovery

The therapeutic techniques the counselor offers to patients must help them to stay in recovery. This occurs by:

- *Creating hope:* Offer encouragement that things will get better.

- *Bonding:* Help the patient to realize they are not alone.

- *Education:* Give the patient an opportunity to learn about illness, symptoms, and behaviors from group members.

- *Altruism:* Assist the patient to learn they have much to offer in terms of helping others, as this will boost self-esteem.

- *Initiating lost connections:* Encourage patients to reconnect with important people lost due to the addiction, such as friends and family.

- *Resolving conflicts:* Take steps to resolve any conflicts with the people who reconnect by sitting in and offering positive monitoring.

- *Developing social skills:* Help the patient to listen and take part in different group activities in order to improve or reconnect with their social skills, such as taking part in role playing activities.

- *Copying actions:* Group therapy members will see positive behaviors among some other group members and want to copy and mimic these behaviors.

- *Personal development:* Behavior outside of a group will surface while taking part in group activities. This will allow the counselor to address behavioral patterns causing a negative impact on the patient's well-being.

- *Expression:* Discuss events and feelings as the main focus of the therapy group. The counselor must work to encourage positive emotional expression.

- *Subconscious feelings:* Patients will have deep fears and hidden feelings arise, which allow them to be addressed and worked through.

- *Goals of therapy:* Goals must be created on a group basis and personal level. Personal goals are attributed to what the patient is looking to gain, while a therapy group should have one common goal in mind.

- *Develop trust for own feelings:* By expressing emotions, discussing them and getting positive feedback, paients will be able to recognize and trust their own feelings more.

- *Trust for others:* Discussing emotions and relating to therapy group members will allow each member to slowly gain trust with others.

- *Develop appropriate confrontational confrontation techniques:* Allow recovering addicts to learn how to express negative feelings to others in a positive manner that leads to resolutions.

- *Develop behavior plan changes:* By expressing emotions and seeing the same emotions within group members, the patient will begin to recognize negative behavior patterns in his or her life and develop a plan to change them.

- *Develop a support group:* This is essential for recovery. Connecting with other positive members and the counselor will allow the recovering addict to develop a strong support group that can aid them through their recovery.

Group Skills Exhibited by Counselors

- Manage and resolve conflicts that occur within the group.

- Stop the formation of small social groups within the larger groups.

- Use appropriate measures in order to deal with difficult group members.

- Address the occurrence of a relapse.

- Provide positive support to group members.

- Continue to educate members on recovery, as well as tools and tips for staying clean on an ongoing basis.

- Work to create cohesion within groups.

Crisis Intervention and Resolution

- Create a helping resolution with the patient.

- Secure a safe environment for the patient and other group members.

- Determine the cause of the crises, such as conflict or loss of family member.

- Offer support to the patient.

- Offer the patient additional resources to cope with cause of crisis.

- Help the patient to create a plan for action during the time of distress.

Immediate Crisis Intervention Steps

1. Initiate the intervention.

2. Offer hope to the patient with positive statements.

3. Provide support to the recovering addict.

4. Provide a solution to problem immediately.

5. Give feedback to the patient in a positive manner.

Individual counseling offers patients the ability to work on a one-on-one basis with a counselor. This form of treatment can offer the recovering addict the ability to express deep issues and concerns that he or she may not feel comfortable expressing in a group setting. The counselor can also provide the patient with a sense of security during individual counseling, which will help the patient acknowledge and address issues they may be afraid to confront. If individual counseling is used along with group therapy, behaviors and traits shown by the member during the group session can be addressed during the individual therapy sessions.

Counselor Services

- *Provide active listening:* Provide the patient with feedback to what he or she tells you, ask questions, develop goals with the patient, and reflect on thoughts and emotions displayed by the patient.

- *Offer empathy:* Put yourself in the patient's shoes in order to develop a true understanding of addiction and related problems.

- *Teach coping skills:* Offer the patient techniques he or she can use to cope with different obstacles in a positive manner.

- *Use paraphrasing:* Repeat important information given by patient so that he or she can hear what they said and reflect on it.

- *Reflection:* Encourage reflection often on thoughts, feelings, and what has been learned so far through counseling. This allows the patient to develop his or her own emotional connection.

- *Avoid interpretation:* Allow the patient to have freedom of expression and don't try to assume feelings they may be having.

- *Offer simplicity:* Take complex issues the patient is facing and offer simple solutions to resolve the conflict.

- *Summarize:* During the end of the session, summarize a reflection on what was discussed, what was learned, and what will occur to expand on these topics during the next session.

- *Use cues:* Use verbal and physical cues in the form of body language to show a patient that you are actively listening to what he or she is telling you.

- *Ask questions:* Leave questions open-ended in order to encourage the patient to explain things in further detail and develop a deeper understanding.

Goal of Individual Counseling

The overall goal of individual counseling is to address the issues causing addiction to occur, and then slowly work through each with an overall goal in mind of creating lasting change. The steps used in process of change will allow the counselor to work with the patient to help them recognize the need for change in certain areas of life, start the process of creating a plan for change, implement the change, and then, through recovery of abuse and underlying issues, allow for lasting change.

Certain issues need to be addressed when working with patients during individual counseling. Some recovering addicts have certain cultural beliefs, outlooks on addiction, and personal beliefs that can affect the treatment plan. Taking each difference into consideration and monitoring the effectiveness of the overall treatment plan throughout the process will allow changes to be made when necessary to make the plan effective.

Methods of Individual Therapy

There are a few different methods used in individual therapy. The method used is based upon the patient's unique needs.

1. *Talk therapy:* This form of treatment creates a secure aenvironment where the patient can discuss his or her issues in confidence, and the therapist can offer encouragement, support, and positive coping techniques.

2. *Cognitive therapy*: This type of therapy uses different methods to encourage the patient to take part in activities designed to change overall thinking, behavior, and ways of handling issues throughout the recovery process.

3. *Hypnosis/EMDR:* While less commonly used, these approaches are designed to change the patient's subconscious mind though special techniques. Some professionals feel these two methods can offer lasting change, because they can help the patient deal with issues they were not aware existed.

Initial Assessment

During the initial assessment, the drug and alcohol counselor will consider different factors in order to determine the patient's best interest. Certain special-needs patients, such as those with mental health issues, may need to be assessed more thoroughly because of certain issues with truth regarding recovery, and the risk of relapse due to the patient stopping his or her medication. With the use of the assessment, the counselor can examine the patient's current and prior history of use, methods for recovery, and what techniques the patient responded to in the past.

Individual counseling may be short- or long-term, based upon the patient's particular case. Generally, the use of drug and alcohol counseling will be provided to the patient until he or she has made substantial progress in the recovery. After this, regular maintenance therapy may be used in order to help the patient to cope with life troubles, as well as to re-examine recovery.

The Attributes of an Individual Counselor

Counseling is a collaborative process that facilitates the client's progress toward mutually determined treatment goals and objectives. Counseling includes methods that are sensitive to individual client characteristics and to the influence of significant others, as well as the client's cultural and social context. Competence in counseling is built upon an understanding of, appreciation of, and ability to appropriately use the contributions of various addiction counseling models as they apply to modalities of care for individuals, groups, families, couples, and significant others. With individual counseling, you must establish a helping relationship with the client characterized by warmth, respect, genuineness, concreteness, and empathy.

Knowledge

- Theories, research, and best-practice literature.
- Approaches to counseling that have demonstrated effectiveness with substance use disorders.
- Definitions of warmth, respect, genuineness, concreteness, and empathy.
- Role of the counselor.
- Therapeutic uses of power and authority.
- Transference, counter-transference, and projective identification.

- Theory and research related to client motivation.

- Alternative theories and methods for motivating clients in a culturally appropriate manner.

- Theory, research, and best practice literature.

- Counseling strategies that promote and support successful client engagement.

- Stages-of-change models used in engagement and treatment strategies.

- Client's culture.

- Assessment and treatment planning.

- Stages of change and recovery.

- The information, skills, and attitudes consistent with recovery.

- Client's goals, treatment plan, prognosis, and motivational level.

- Assessment methods to measure progress toward positive change.

- Counseling theory, treatment and practice literature as it applies to substance use disorders.

- Relapse prevention theory, practice, and outcome literature.

- Behaviors and cognition consistent with the development, maintenance, and attainment of treatment goals.

- Counseling treatment methods that support positive client behaviors consistent with recovery.

- Client history and treatment plan.

- Client behaviors that are inconsistent with the recovery process.

- Behavioral and cognitive therapy literature about substance use disorders.

- Cognitive, behavioral, and pharmacological interventions appropriate for relapse prevention.

- Theory, research, and outcome-based literature demonstrating the importance of significant others, including families and other social systems, to treatment progress.

- Social and family systems theory.

- How to apply appropriate confidentiality regulations.

- Client and system worldviews relative to health..

- How infectious diseases are transmitted and prevented.

- The relationship between lifestyles and infectious diseases.

- Harm reduction concepts, research, and methods.

- Basic and life skills associated with recovery.

- Theory, research, and practice literature that examines the relationship of basic and life skills to the attainment of positive treatment outcomes.

- Tools used to determine levels of basic and life skills.

- Impact of culture on substance use.

- Cultural factors affecting responsiveness to varying counseling strategies.

- Current research concerning differences in drinking and substance use patterns based on the characteristics of the client.

- Addiction counseling strategies.

- How to apply appropriate strategies based on the client's treatment plan.

- Client's family and social systems and relationships between each.

- Client and system's cultural norms, biases, and preferences.

- Literature relating spirituality to addiction and recovery.

- Client behaviors that tend to be inconsistent with recovery.

- The client's social and life circumstances.

- Relapse prevention strategies.

- Therapeutic interventions.

- Differences between crisis intervention and other kinds of therapeutic intervention.

- Characteristics of a serious crisis and typical reactions.

- Post-traumatic stress and other relevant psychiatric disorders.

- Roles played by loved ones in crisis development and/or reaction.

- Relationship of crisis to client's stage of change.

- Client's usual coping strategies.

- Steps to aid in crisis resolution, including determination of what client can do on his/her own and what must be done by counselor, family, or significant others in client system.

Skills

- Active listening, including paraphrasing, reflecting, and summarizing.

- Conveying warmth, respect, and genuineness in an appropriate manner.

- Demonstrating empathic understanding.

- Using power and authority appropriately in support of treatment goals.

- Implementing appropriate engagement and interviewing approaches.

- Assessing client readiness for change.

- Using culturally appropriate counseling strategies.

- Assessing the client's responses to therapeutic interventions.

- Formulating and documenting concise, descriptive, and measurable treatment outcome statements.

- Teaching the client to identify goals and formulate action plans.

- Motivational techniques.

- Recognizing client strengths.

- Assessing and providing feedback on client progress toward treatment goals.

- Assessing life and basic skills and comprehension levels of client and all significant others associated with the treatment plan.

- Identification and documentation of change.

- Coaching, mentoring, and teaching.

- Recognizing and addressing ambivalence and resistance.

- Using behavioral and cognitive methods that reinforce positive client behaviors.

- Using objective observation and documentation.

- Assessing and re-assessing client behaviors.

- Monitoring the client's behavior for consistency with preferred treatment outcomes.

- Presenting inconsistencies between client behaviors and goals.

- Re-framing and redirecting negative behaviors.

- Conflict resolution, decision-making, and problem solving skills.

- Recognizing and addressing underlying client issues that may impede treatment progress.

- Identifying the client's family and social systems .

- Recognizing the impact of the client's family and social systems on the treatment process.

- Engaging significant others in the treatment process.

- Using a repertoire of techniques that, based on an assessment of various client and system characteristics, will promote and reinforce health-enhancing activities.

- Coaching, mentoring, and teaching techniques relative to the promotion and maintenance of health.

- Demonstrating cultural competence in discussing sexuality.

- Teaching life skills appropriate to the client's situation and skill level.

- Applying assessment tools to determine the client's level of basic and life skills.

- Communicating how basic and life skills relate to treatment outcomes.

- Individualizing treatment plans.

- Adapting counseling strategies to unique client characteristics and circumstances.

- Practicing cultural communication.

- Monitoring client progress.

- Using various methods to present inconsistencies between client's behaviors and treatment goals.

- Re-framing and redirecting negative behaviors.

- Utilizing appropriate intervention strategies.

- Carrying out steps in crisis resolution.

- Assessing and engaging client and client system strengths and resources.

- Assessing for immediate concerns regarding safety and any potential harm to others.

- Making appropriate referrals as necessary.

- Assessing and acting upon issues of confidentiality that may be part of crisis response.

- Assisting the client to ventilate emotions and normalize feelings.

Attitudes

- Respect for the client.
- Recognition of the importance of cooperation and collaboration with the client.
- Professional objectivity.
- Facilitation of the client's engagement in the treatment and recovery process.
- Respect for the client's frame of reference.
- Work with the client to establish realistic, achievable goals consistent with achieving and maintaining recovery.
- Appreciation for the client's resources and preferences.
- Appreciation for individual differences in the treatment and recovery process.
- Promote client knowledge, skills, and attitudes that contribute to a positive change in substance use behaviors.
- Genuine care and concern for client, family, and significant others.
- Appreciation for incremental change.
- Patience and perseverance.
- Encourage and reinforce client actions determined to be beneficial in progressing toward treatment goals.
- Therapeutic optimism.
- Patience and perseverance.
- Appreciation for incremental changes.
- Work appropriately with the client to recognize and discourage all behaviors inconsistent with progress toward treatment goals.
- Patience and perseverance during periods of treatment difficulty.
- Accepting relapse as an opportunity for positive change.
- Recognizing the value of a constructive helping relationship.
- Recognize how, when, and why to involve the client's significant others in enhancing or supporting the treatment plan.

- Appreciation for the need of significant others to be involved in the client's treatment plan, within the bounds of confidentiality.

- Respect for the contribution of significant others to the treatment process.

- Promote client knowledge, skills, and attitudes consistent with the maintenance of health and prevention of human immunodeficiency virus/acquired immune deficiency syndrome (HIV/AIDS), tuberculosis (TB), sexually transmitted diseases (STDs), and other infectious diseases.

- Openness to discussions about health issues, lifestyle, and sexuality.

- Recognition of the counselor's potential to model a healthy life-style.

- Facilitate the development of basic and life skills associated with recovery.

- Recognizing that recovery involves a broader life context than the elimination of symptoms.

- Accepting relapse as an opportunity for learning and/or skills acquisition.

- Adapt counseling strategies to the individual characteristics of the client, including but not limited to, disability, gender, sexual orientation, developmental level, culture, ethnicity, age, and health status.

- Recognition of the need for flexibility in meeting client needs.

- Willingness to adjust strategies in accordance with client's characteristics.

- A non-judgmental, respectful acceptance of cultural, behavioral, and value differences.

- Constructive therapeutic responses to unproductive behavior.

- Therapeutic optimism.

- Perseverance during periods of treatment difficulty.

- Apply crisis management skills.

- Recognize crisis as an opportunity for change.

- Confidence in the midst of crisis.

- Recognize personal and professional limitations.

- Facilitate the client's identification, selection, and practice of strategies that help sustain the knowledge, skills, and attitudes needed for maintaining treatment progress and preventing relapse.

- Recognize that clients must assume responsibility for their own recovery.

Vocational Rehabilitation

Vocational rehabilitation allows the recovering addict to overcome barriers to accessing and maintaining employment or a useful occupation. This may require several mental health professionals like disability advisers and career counselors.

Techniques used For Vocational Rehabilitation

- Goal setting
- Intervention planning
- Providing of health advice and promotion
- Support for self-management of recovery
- Psychosocial interventions
- Career counseling, job analysis, and placement services
- Functional capacity evaluations

Determining Rehabilitation Readiness

A recovering addict will show readiness for vocational rehabilitation when he or she:
- Recognizes abuse and involvement in the treatment program.
- Shows commitment to recovery.
- Shows progress towards achievement of goals and areas of employment.
- Shows ongoing sobriety.
- Addresses entry issues as part of a better life goal plan.
- Understands why vocational rehabilitation is needed.
- Addresses entry issues as part of a better life call.
- Understands why vocational rehabilitation is an effective program for maintaining sobriety.
- Is able to independently complete process keeping a job.

Vocational Rehabilitation Services

- *Referral* - Clients can be self-referred or referred by the rehabilitation institution, family, or physicians.

- *Application* - The vocational rehabilitation service counselor gathers and evaluates information to determine work eligibility. This involves an assessment of the physical and/or mental impairment.

- *Extended evaluation* - When additional information is needed to determine work eligibility, the counselor may need additional time to determine disability and possibilities.

Rehabilitation Program Development

The counselor and client must both determine a job that will allow the client to reach certain goals. The job goal and other objectives are specified in an Individualized Plan for Employment (IPE). Services may include:

- Vocational guidance and counseling

- Mental health treatment to correct or modify an impairment

- Training (vocational school or on-the-job)

- Rehabilitation technology (assistive devices)

- Placement assistance and follow-up

Vocational and Habilitation Options

- *Supported Employment (SE)* - This involves a situation where persons with severe disabilities are placed in positions with qualified job coaches who provide ongoing support services so the client can retain employment.

- *Independent Living Services (ILS)* - These services promote independent living, including client control, self-help, peer support, equal access, and system advocacy. These things are done to maximize the integration and inclusion of the person into the community with independence and productivity.

With group counseling, the counselor describes, selects, and appropriately uses strategies from accepted and culturally appropriate models for group counseling.

The Attributes of a Group Counselor

Knowledge

- A variety of group methods appropriate to achieving client objectives in a treatment population.

- Research concerning the effectiveness of varying models and strategies for group counseling with general populations.

- Research concerning the effectiveness of varying models and strategies for populations with substance use disorders.

- Research and theory concerning the effectiveness of varying models and strategies for group counseling with members of varying cultural groups.

- Therapeutic use of humor.

- Specific group models and strategies relative to client's age, gender, cultural context.

- Selection criteria, methods, and instruments for screening and selecting group members.

- General principles for selecting group goals, outcomes, and ground rules.

- General principles for appropriately graduating group members and terminating groups.

- Developmental processes affecting therapeutic groups over time.

- Issues faced by individuals and the group as a whole upon entry of new members.

- Issues faced by individuals and by the group as a whole upon exit of members.

- Characteristics of transition stages in therapeutic groups.

- Characteristics of therapeutic group behavior.

- Leadership, facilitator, and counseling methods appropriate for each group type and therapeutic setting.

- Types and uses of power and authority in therapeutic group process.
- Stages of group development and counseling methods appropriate to each stage.
- Definitions of the concepts of process and content.
- Difference between the group process and the content of the discussion.
- Methods and techniques of group problem solving, decision-making, and addressing group conflict.
- How process variables affect the group's ability to focus on content concerns.
- How content variables affect the group's ability to focus on process concerns.

Skills

- Designing and implementing strategies to meet the needs of specific groups.
- Recognizing and accommodating appropriate individual needs within the group.
- Leading therapeutic groups for clients with substance use disorders.
- Using humor appropriately.
- Conducting screening interviews.
- Assessing individual client's appropriateness for participation in group.
- Using group process to negotiate group goals, outcomes, and ground rules within the context of the individual needs and objectives of group members.
- Using group process to negotiate appropriate criteria and methods for transition to the next appropriate level of care.
- Adapting group counseling skills as appropriate for group type.
- Using group process to prepare group members for transition and to resolve transitional issues.
- Effectively dealing with different types of resistant behaviors, transference, and countertransference issues.
- Recognizing when members are ready to exit.
- Applying group counseling methods leading to measurable progress toward group and individual goals and outcomes.

- Recognizing when and how to use appropriate power.

- Documenting measurable progress toward group and individual goals.

- Observing and documenting process and content.

- Assessing when to make appropriate process interventions.

- Using strategies congruent with enhancing both process and content in order to meet individual and group goals.

- Recognizing that a client's behavior can be, but is not always, reflective of the client's treatment needs.

- Documenting client's group behavior that has implications for treatment planning.

- Recognizing the similarities and differences between individual needs and group processes.

- Redesigning individual treatment plans based on the observation of group behaviors.

Attitudes

- Openness and flexibility in the choice of counseling strategies that meet needs of the group and the individuals within the group.

- Recognition of the value of the use of groups as an effective therapeutic intervention.

- Carry out the actions necessary to form a group, including, but not limited to: determining group type, purpose, size, and leadership; recruiting and selecting members; establishing group goals and clarifying behavioral ground rules for participating; identifying outcomes; and determining criteria and methods for termination or graduation from the group.

- Recognition of the importance of involving group members in the establishment of group goals, outcomes, ground rules, and graduation and termination criteria.

- Recognition of the fact that the nature of the specific group model should depend on the needs, goals, outcomes, and cultural context of the participants.

- Facilitate the entry of new members and the transition of exiting members.

- Recognition of the need to balance individual needs with group needs, goals, and outcomes.

- Appreciation for the contribution of new and continuing group members in the group process.

- Maintaining non-judgmental attitudes and behaviors.

- Respect for the emotional experience of the entry and exit of group members on the rest of the group.

- Facilitate group growth within the established ground rules and movement toward group and individual goals by using methods consistent with group type.

- Recognition of the value of the use of different group counseling methods and leadership or facilitation styles.

- Appreciation for the role and power of the group facilitator.

- Appreciation for the role and power of various group members in the group process.

- Understand the concepts of process and content, and shift the focus of the group when such an intervention will help the group move toward its goals.

- Appreciating the appropriate use of content and process interventions.

- Describe and summarize client behavior within the group for the purpose of documenting the client's progress and identifying needs and issues that may require a modification in the treatment plan.

- Recognition of the value of accurate documentation.

- Appreciation of individual differences in rates of progress towards treatment goals and use of group intervention.

Counseling for Families, Couples, and Significant Others

To counsel families, couples, and significant others, the counselor must understand the characteristics and dynamics of families, couples, and significant others affected by substance use.

Knowledge

- Dynamics associated with substance use, abuse, and dependence in families, couples, and significant others.

- Impact of interaction patterns on substance use behaviors.

- Cultural factors related to the impact of substance use disorders on families, couples, and significant others.

- Systems theory and dynamics.

- Signs and patterns of domestic violence.

- Impacts of substance use behaviors on interaction patterns.

- Intervention strategies appropriate for systems at varying stages of problem development and resolution.

- Intervention strategies appropriate for violence against persons.

- Laws and resource regarding violence against persons.

- Culturally appropriate family intervention strategies.

- Appropriate and available assessment tools for use with families, couples, and significant others.

- How to apply appropriate confidentiality regulations.

- Methods for engaging members of the family, couple, or significant others to focus on their own concerns when the substance abuser is not ready to participate.

- The impact of family interaction patterns on substance use.

- The impact of substance use on family interaction patterns.

- Theory and research literature outlining systemic interventions in psychoactive substance abuse situations, including violence against persons.

- Healthy behavioral patterns for families, couples, and significant others.

- Empirically based systemic counseling strategies associated with recovery.

- Stages of recovery for families, couples, and significant others.

Skills

- Identifying systemic interactions that are likely to affect recovery.

- Recognizing the roles of significant others within the client's social system.

- Recognizing potential for and signs and symptoms of domestic violence.

- Applying assessment tools for use with families, couples, and significant others.

- Applying culturally appropriate intervention strategies.

- Working within the bounds of confidentiality regulations.

- Identifying goals based on both individual and systemic concerns.

- Using appropriate therapeutic interventions with system members that address established treatment goals.

- Describing systemic issues constructively to families, couples, and significant others.

- Teaching system members to identify and interrupt harmful interaction patterns.

- Helping system members practice and evaluate alternate interaction patterns.

- Assisting system members to identify and practice behaviors designed to resolve the crises brought about by changes in substance use behaviors.

- Assisting family members to identify and practice behaviors associated with long-term maintenance of healthy interactions.

Attitudes

- Recognition of non-constructive family behaviors as systemic issues.

- Appreciation of the role systemic interactions plays in substance use behavior.

- Appreciation for diverse cultural factors that influence characteristics and dynamics of families, couples and significant others.

- Be familiar with and appropriately use models of diagnosis and intervention for families, couples, and significant others, including extended, kinship, or tribal family structures.

- Recognition of the validity of viewing the system as the client, while respecting the rights and needs of individuals.

- Appreciation for the diversity found in families, couples, and significant others.

- Facilitate the engagement of selected members of the family, couple, or significant others in the treatment and recovery process.

- Recognition of the usefulness of working with those individual systems members who are personally ready to participate in the counseling process.

- Respect for confidentiality regulations.

- Assist families, couples, and significant others to understand the interaction between the family system and substance use behaviors.

- Appreciation for the complexities of counseling families, couples, and significant others.

- Assist families, couples, and significant others to adopt strategies and behaviors that sustain recovery and maintain healthy relationships.

- Appreciation for a variety of approaches in working with families, couples, and significant others.

Health Issues

User training, knowledge, and skills regarding STDs help educate the recovering addict regarding transmission. To apply this in a group or one-on-one setting, the counselor will need to gain experience. In some cases, counselors train alongside mentors and work to apply theory to real-world settings. This includes:

- Recognize all physical signs of STDs that can occur with a patient. This can include lesions on the skin, bruising, fevers, persistent coldness, and other similar attributes.

- Provide the group with education on the risk of infection.

- Instruct on ways the person could prevent transmission to another individual.

- Offer appropriate coping skills to the group during this experiment.

- Explain treatment methods that are used for different types of STDs.

- Determine display of risky behavior that is present within the group.

Experiential Therapy

Experiential therapy is a form of psychotherapy that allows clients to discover and address subconscious and hidden issues through various experiences, such as guided imagery, role-playing, the use of props and other activities. This therapy emphasizes taking personal responsibility and is a category rather than one specific type of therapy. Examples of experiential therapy include equine, recreation, expressive art, wilderness, adventure, and music therapy. Experiential therapy is a useful tool for clients to examine personal relationships and how each relationship affects his or her current behavior. Clients with drug and alcohol addictions can see how negative emotions trigger compulsive behaviors. The client is able to participate and recreate situations that trigger difficult emotions and feelings so these may be addressed.

Emotions are a direct reflection of a person's personal reality. They tell the individual's story of his or her life, regardless of how good or bad that may be. This helps participants locate and decipher emotions that have been stored away. Clients can experience negative episodes from the past, and this allows them to identify the emotions related to those episodes. Once this occurs, the client can create solutions to resolve the damage and promote self-healing.

Examples of Experiential Therapy

- Psychodrama
- Recreation therapy
- Music therapy
- Equine therapy
- Adventure therapy
- Wilderness therapy
- Expressive art therapy

Benefits of Experiential Therapy

There are numerous benefits and advantages of experiential therapy. These include:

- Provides opportunities for the counselor to observe the client in situations where the client is not focused on the therapy.

- Allows recovery under the supervision of a qualified, skilled therapist.

- Develops improved self-esteem.

- Allows the recovering addict to take responsibility for his or her actions.

- Is a personal empowerment and emotional growth experience.

Family and Addiction

Overview of Family and Addiction Issues

The recovering addict's family plays an important role in both the active addiction and recovery process. According to addiction experts, these people may take part in the use, abuse, or overuse of substances and enable the patient to continue using. There are two functions in family addiction:

- Primary causes and issues with the patient's well-being, functioning, and level of recovery.

- Therapy used to resolve family issues from the past. It is used to determine how abuse affects each member in the family.

Therapy Benefits

- Works to create change within the family structure.

- Creates techniques that help to reach higher levels of function.

- Provides strength to the members of the family.

- Offers different coping techniques to family members.

Types of Families

- *Functional* – The family system is stable and the user is typically in the early stages of addiction.

- *Neurotic enmeshed* – Abuse is considered a symptom/cause of the family dynamics/dysfunction. Communication is poor, and fighting is common.

- *Disintegrated* – There is some temporary separation between the substance user and the family members. This is when a neurotic enmeshed family progresses to a later stage of the addiction.

- *Absent* – With this family type, there is permanent separation between the addict and the members of the family.

Counseling Techniques

- *Joining:* The ability to connect, understand, and build strength within families. This is stabilized by helping the patient stop abuse by creating goals within the family. This helps the recovering addict see how his or her behavior change affects the family.

- *Education:* Addiction and resources are provided to the patient and family members. In addition, the recovering addict can utilize outside resources in order to continue on a successful recovery path.

- *Structured analysis:* Determine reasons why a family does not work, examine problems, and figure out a solution for better family dynamics.

- *Alternative coping techniques:* Teach honest demonstration of feelings to family members so that they can express their emotions and determine how they can use them to solve problems.

- *Relapse prevention:* Plan to prevent and cope in the event of a relapse; this can include the family's ability to prevent relapse.

- *Drug substitution:* This is the substitution of a legal drug for an illegal one to assist the patient in making positive changes. An example of this would be a methadone program.

Verbal, physical, and psychological abuse all are used by family members against each other. Many studies have shown that violence and addiction go hand-in-hand - over one-half of men convicted of battery have addiction issues.

The actual use of drugs and alcohol has not been established as the *cause* of the abuse – rather, substance abuse is a learned technique. Violence is used to control the victim. Many women who are subjected to abuse use drugs in order to cope with the abuse. Additionally, they may seek partners who have addiction problems of their own. Counselors must determine the dynamics that surround use and abuse by family members.

Domestic Violence Diagnosis and Assessment

Women are convicted every year of domestic violence offenses, but it is more common for men to be the abuser in a heterosexual relationship. During the process of treatment, the counselor must interview both the victim and abuser in order to gain a complete understanding of the abuse present within the relationship. Diagnosis and assessment of domestic violence involves:

- Discovering family dynamics revolving around addiction and abuse.

- Identifying issues within the family in order to evaluate and treat them.

- Examining each person's beliefs regarding family issues.

Three Common Myths about Battering

- *Myth: Battering is a disease.*
  Truth: The batterer abuses because they suffer from low self-esteem.

- *Myth: Loss of emotion is a direct cause of battering.*
  Truth: Abusers know it is wrong, but they batter in order to feel better about themselves.

- *Myth: Battering occurs due to lack of self-control.*
  Truth: Abuse is a learned behavior, and many times, the person abusing will have suffered abuse in the past, and now uses it to gain control.

Techniques Used for Domestic Violence Treatment

While the techniques used for domestic violence treatment vary based on each unique case, there are a variety of techniques used within domestic violence cases that have proven effective. These techniques are used to address the issue of abuse, examine how it relates to the addiction, and determine steps to stop the abuse from occurring in the future. Some of the most effective techniques include:

- *Funneling* - This is used as a process to determine how each person within the relationship views abuse, done during individual or couple sessions. This information is generally revealed over time in small pieces.

- *Interviewing* - The counselor must interview each member of the family separately in order to allow each person to speak freely about their feelings regarding different issues of abuse and addiction.

- *Emotional* expression - Ask both partners to specify if they feel that the abuse is justified, and if so, why? This allows the counselor to examine underlying issues within the patient that may be difficult to see on the surface, such as low self-esteem in a patient who makes excuses for their abusive partner.

- *Be assertive* - The counselor must be direct with a questioning process for the patient, the abuser, or the victim during the time of the questioning.

- *Detect* – Determine if the abuser or victim is making excuses, and address and explore these excuses. *Eliminate blaming* - Stop blaming the use of a substance for the cause of the battery.

- *Provide education* - Educate both abuser and victim on substance abuse, and how it is not the cause of battering.

- *Analyze level of abuse* - If the abuse is considered to be a danger to the patient, the counselor must take the proper steps in order to protect the patient from serious, impending harm.

- *Incorporate proper therapy sessions* - Work with patients alone and together in order to develop a nonviolence plan. If patient is the abuser, the counselor must help them create a non-violence plan in order to stop him or her from becoming violent during times of aggression.

- *Examine different areas* - Examine all aspects of the abuse in terms of the feelings that are associated, the amount and when it occurs.

- *Determine results* - Determine how substance abuse plays a role in couple dynamics. For example, does substance abuse occur during the time of battery, prior to, or after? While getting answers to these questions, examine and address feelings associated with violence.

- *Monitor behavior* - Examine behavioral changes within the patient during the time of the interview, and develop appropriate coping strategies to change the behaviors.

- *Provide resources* - Refer the patient to self-help groups, as this will help them to cope with the abuse by developing peers, support, and coping skills. These things help them to modify and change the behavior on a long-term basis.

Three Stages in the Cycle of Abuse

1. *Increased tension* - An increase in the amount of tension that occurs within the household.

2. *Violence* – The situation becomes violent in the form of physical or psychological abuse.

3. *Compensation* - The abuser may become apologetic. Once forgiven, or forgotten, the cycle will almost always start back at stage one. It's important to teach the victim this cycle and how to watch for increased tension again.

Research has proven that the main risk periods for drug abuse are during major transitions in the life of the adolescent. The first major transition is leaving a secure environment (such as middle or high school), and entering another school. This is when adolescents are likely to encounter drugs for the first time. Adolescents face many emotional, social, and educational challenges during high school, so there is more exposure and availability of drugs. A greater risk occurs when young adults leave home to attend college or work on their own for the first time.

During the last 20 years, researchers have attempted to determine how drug use begins during adolescence and how it progresses. Several risk factors add to a person's propensity for substance abuse, but protective factors reduce it.

Risk Factors

- Low parental supervision
- Limited communication with parents
- Family conflicts
- Inconsistent or severe parental discipline
- Family history of drug and alcohol use
- Sexual victimization
- Learning or emotional problems
- Emotional instability
- Thrill-seeking behaviors
- Poor social coping skills
- Affiliations of peers who display deviant behaviors

Protective Factors

- Strong and positive family bonds
- Parental monitoring of teen's activities
- Parental involvement
- Success in school performance

- Strong bond with religious organization
- Clear rules of conduct that are enforced

Testing Methods

A counselor may administer tests to determine an adolescent's propensity for substance abuse or current level of substance abuse.

Professional Experience Questionnaire

- 40-question testing process.

- Fourth-grade level of education testing

- Examines levels of addiction severity

- Examines psychological and behavioral issues involved in the addiction process

- Examines personal and environmental issues

- Determines age and the frequency of substance use

SaSSI Testing

- Distinguishes between use and abuse

- Age test used for persons aged 12 years and older

- 70-question testing process

- Used to determine types of treatment available

- Present with or without psychological issues

Counseling Adolescents

The way that addiction affects the adolescent can vary based on different aspects regarding the child, such as his or her temperament, or the level of negative occurrences that result within the family due to the addiction. In order to determine how the addiction is affecting the child, the following steps should be taken:

- Ask how family members' addiction affects the adolescent.

- Determine how both the adolescent and the user may play a role within the addiction process. It is important to assure the adolescent that he or she is not responsible for the addiction, but that they can take measures to ensure they are not enabling a family member who is abusing drugs or alcohol.

- Create a positive and effective plan based on the effects the addiction has on the adolescent and family.

- Develop a recovery plan based on the level of impact of the addiction on the family and the resultant social and emotional problems.

- Determine if the problem faced is the real issue within the family, or if denial of the addiction is the real factor. A continued denial of the addiction will lead to long-term negative effects for the entire family, and this could result in death due to overdose from unintentional enabling by the family.

- When denial of addiction is present, the family must first learn to accept the addiction as a real issue before it can be properly addressed.

Assessment of Substance Abuse, Lethality, and Level of Care

Identification of an individual can be made through many different channels, including self-identification, court order, a condition of one's probation or parole, and/or through intervention techniques. This could involve the screening process used to determine the likelihood that an individual has a problem.

Assessment is the collection of data from individual and corroborative sources to determine the extent of the individual's problem and their strengths, weaknesses, and needs. This information is used to formulate the plan of treatment, to include goals, methods and resources. Assessment is necessary to stabilize the patient in order to prevent serious health issues or death.

Rehabilitation and Treatment Programs

Rehabilitation and treatment programs will vary by setting, with the primary focus on the care of the recovering addict. The continuum of treatment depends on the assessment and diagnosis of the patient and can range from education courses to an inpatient residential program. Substance abuse and associated treatment services should be individualized and appropriate to the needs of the patient.

The continuum of substance abuse and associated services may be provided within a facility by coordinating programming with other facilities, such as a medical facility and sharing arrangements with community resources. Recovering addicts should move along the continuum as is clinically appropriate, with minimal disruption in treatment and in a manner that facilitates positive treatment outcomes.

Case management should be used to ensure that patients receive all necessary services in a timely and coordinated manner. The utilization of individual, group, and family counseling should be utilized as needed to assist in meeting the needs of the patient. All substance abuse programs should be sensitive to the needs of special populations involving the homeless, those with a dual diagnosis, HIV-infected persons, the elderly, ethnic and racial minorities, and both males and females.

Relapse Prevention

Relapse prevention is an important part of treatment from the beginning. Counseling and treatment involve working on problems and concerns that have played a role in the client's behavior. This involves learning to make decisions and choices that do not facilitate relapse. Recovery and relapse are both ongoing processes, not an event, so relapse prevention should be approached with the identification of individualized triggers and a plan to confront those triggers should they occur.

When discussing relapse prevention, talk with the patient about the abstinence violation effect (AVE). The abstinence violation effect refers to the tendency for some people to use substances problematically when they believe abstinence is too difficult a goal to achieve or maintain. AVE relates to what happens when a person attempting to abstain from a negative habitual behavior, such as drug use, engages in the behavior, and then faces conflict and guilt by making internal attributions to explain why he or she did it. This makes the individual more likely to continue using the drug, for instance, in order to cope with self-blame and guilt.

Substance Abuse and Pre-Adolescents

Substance abuse for the pre-adolescent carries a stigma. Issues often seen with children who are part of a household involving addiction include lack of trust, no sense of self-worth, boundary issues, lack of feelings, impulsivity, self-harm and other negative feelings projected on themselves or to others. These children may also experience a feeling of guilt for the person who is abusing drugs or alcohol, which may encourage additional use. When the child ends up feeling bad, it can result in encouraging the parent to use, although the child was trying to create a bonding relationship or to prevent tension.

Recovering addicts, domestic abusers, and victims of abuse must create their own definition of domestic abuse and identify different keywords associated with it. In doing so, they come to understand how they relate to abuse and determine thought patterns that could have a negative impact on the person being treated. While completing this process, the client should:

- Determine how he or she learned to define domestic abuse, such as through television or other media.

- Identify how he or she associates with the terms linked with addiction recovery and abuse.

- After the person has analyzed feelings associated with these terms, he or she can use the definitions in both a negative and positive manner. For negative thoughts regarding different areas of domestic abuse, he or she can recognize these thoughts, learn more about that area of abuse, and then take steps to change thought patterns in a way that will not affect the patient.

- Once the person has positive definitions of certain areas involving domestic violence, such as recovering from violence, the person can use these terms during certain times. While technical terms may be difficult for some people to understand, some can allow the patient to develop an understanding regarding certain areas of their abuse and/or addiction.

- Definitions can be used during both group and individual counseling.

Spirituality, Change and Motivation

Spirituality

It is crucial that discussions of spirituality proceed at the patient's pace and of their volition. A counselor may ask about faith traditions or spirituality, but should not press a patient who is not inclined to discuss it. However, if the patient is willing to discuss religion and spirituality, a counselor may find important components of the addiction and recovery process in the patient's individual beliefs.

Patients suffering from addiction commonly have little or no spirituality. Many times, when addiction has become prolonged, negative, and life changing, the patient can experience a disconnection from themselves and their prior beliefs – or may never have had any to begin with. The patient may also experience a feeling of indifference to the topic of spirituality, or have a hard time connecting with his or her beliefs. One of the most common cases of feeling indifferent to spirituality is due to misunderstanding. Many patients are not familiar with the difference between spirituality and religion, and can mistake them for one concept. When this is the case, certain ideas associated with particular faith traditions can cause indifference or hostility to any concept associated with either religion or spirituality.

The inability to connect with the spiritual self, lack of understanding, and other issues involving this area could lead to difficulties with the patient's spirituality, or a complete lack of spiritual presence. Many studies regarding spirituality have found that this lack can affect the addiction process greatly, because some individuals have a difficult time with recovery if they do not connect with their spirituality.

Issues of Spirituality in Recovery

Some issues seen within recovery regarding spirituality include:

- Lack of any type of spirituality within their lives
- Lack of understanding of how religion is different than spirituality

Spirituality is a component of many addiction treatment programs as part of overall therapy. Issues regarding spirituality are sometimes vitally important to a patient's recovery. The process of treatment based in spirituality is often seen to have similar characteristics as a 12-step program. When discussing spirituality with a patient, remember the following:

- Never push spiritual beliefs on to a patient. There is nothing wrong with a patient choosing atheism or agnosticism.

- Refer the patient to spiritual groups only if he or she wishes.

Many problems of mind, body and spirit spring from addiction – so as the patient undergoes the recovery process, the counselor can help them develop a solid recovery plan based on their individual physical, mental and spiritual characteristics.

A reminder: It is not only unethical for a counselor to push spirituality onto a patient, but can be harmful and counterproductive, instantly destroying carefully constructed trust and positive relationship dynamics. However, during the initial assessment of the patient, and in order to determine what the patient's feelings toward spirituality are, the counselor can assess this aspect of recovery with the consent of the patient.

Addiction experts who study the results of change within patients have discovered that the use of motivational counseling techniques is one of the most effective therapies. Change and motivational counseling can provide lifelong recovery for those affected by addiction.

Change in the Addict

Changes occur when the patient:

- Makes a connection between their life problems and the process of addiction.

- Develops an action plan for use throughout recovery.

- Takes part in interconnected change and self-discovery.

- Develops positive attitudes and maintains them throughout the recovery.

- Maintains hope throughout the recovery process with positive coping skills.

- Continues to keep perspective, even during difficult times.

Stages of Change

1. *Precontemplation* - The patient is not looking for change, and the addiction doesn't seem to be an issue. He or she usually starts to recognize that addiction is present during the precontemplation stage.

2. *Preparation* - The patient plans to make a change, but may have failed in the past, or may have created a plan and failed to actively participate in it. Small, insignificant changes are made by the patient during the preparation stage.

3. *Action* - During this stage, a commitment to change is made. The patient works with the counselor in order to determine different areas of their life that need to be modified, such as behavior and environmental exposure.

4. *Maintenance:* During this stage, changes are maintained for six months or longer.

5. *Termination:* During the fifth stage, major changes are made. Relaxation is no longer an issue for the patient, as he or she continues to be active in recovery. Although termination of the addiction can be achieved with the right mindset, complete termination is difficult to reach, because addiction is often a life-long, ongoing process of change that needs constant maintenance.

The Benefits of Motivational Counseling

- It helps the patient to engage in an early treatment plan.

- Useful when the patient shows resistance to change during the process of treatment with the counselor.

The Phases of Motivational Counseling

- *Empathy* - During this phase, the counselor positively accepts the patient, creates a comfortable environment, acts with genuine concern and kindness, and focuses on learning about the patient and his or her prior history (not only with abuse, but in other areas of life that have affected well-being). The empathy process invites and allows for permanent change.

- *Discrepancy* - Often paired with self-sufficient and empathetic processes. It helps the patient to determine what areas need to be addressed. The counselor will work with the patient in order to help him or her develop love and trust in the self. This can be done by developing external and internal support. Discrepancy helps the patient to see that change is possible, and helps the patient become less likely to rationalize or project areas of change.

- *Resistance* - Preventative steps are taken by the counselor to help avoid power struggle during this stage. The spirit of motivational counseling must be present during all sessions in order for this therapy to be effective and for the recovery process to be successful.

All human beings are individuals who are shaped by a confluence of environmental, individual, experiential and cultural factors. There are no "silver bullet" treatment plans for all white males any more than there are one-size-fits-all treatment plans for black women. Every individual is different, and stereotypes do not serve a counselor's quest to help a patient in their recovery process. However, it is important for the counselor to be aware of elements commonly found in cultures, mores, norms, relational statuses to majority populations and societal expectations within specific populations.

Gender-appropriate and culturally responsive counseling improves long-term outcomes for patients. The risks of substance abuse differ by race, gender, sexual orientation, age, ethnicity, and other factors. These disorders also involve education, economic status, geographic location, and culture. Understanding special populations is critical for implementing an effective substance abuse therapy plan.

Latino/Latina

There are around 40 million Latino/Latina people in the U.S., most of whom are Mexican-American. The socioeconomic status of many members of this population reflects circumstances of recent immigration or being the first natural born citizen in a family of immigrants. In a recent survey of Hispanic/Latino men and women, 33 percent of men and 12 percent of women admitted to heavy drinking. The main substances used among Hispanic people are opiates and crack/cocaine.

Treatment programs for Latinos and Latinas sometimes focus on developing services that endorse culturally competent practices and create an environment that honors their heritage and incorporates certain appropriate cultural values. Substance abuse counseling based on a family model is often effective - additionally, gender roles are often important, with emphasis on aspects of "marianisimo" and "machismo" such as strength, flexibility, and the ability to survive.

African-American

This highest population density of African Americans is in Southern states and in cities around the country. The largest racial minority in America, at 12.1% of the population, many black people experience legacy poverty resulting from centuries of institutionalized racism, and still suffer its lasting socioeconomic effects, such as difficulty accessing quality education, being fairly treated in regards to employment, and securing housing outside of high-crime, low-property-value neighborhoods. Substance use among this special population has been in decline since the 1990s, though recent studies indicate that alcohol use accounts for around 25 percent of treatment admissions for African American women. Around 35 percent of admissions to treatment facilities for African Americans in general are for cocaine abuse.

It is necessary for African Americans to have access to services that provide adequate social support during addiction recovery. They often are at risk for substance use due to exposure to economic stressors and biopsychosocial issues that lead to coping difficulties and emotional distress. From a racial standpoint, African Americans bear a disproportionate burden of heterosexual HIV infection, a fact the counselor should bring up any time a black patient admits to drug use by injection. Treatments often found to be effective involve social networks, family therapy, and community involvement.

Asian and Pacific American

Asian origins include countries such as India, China, Cambodia, Japan, Korea, Vietnam, and the Philippines. More than 7 million Asian and Pacific Americans live in America. This group represents one percent of admissions to substance abuse treatment centers, but this number has increased in the last decade. Due to many Asian-Americans lacking a genetic enzyme that breaks down alcohol, they often are especially vulnerable to alcohol intoxication and much more severe aftereffects than many other racial populations. Thus, Asian-Americans have the lowest percentage of current alcohol problems or histories of alcohol abuse. The rates of illicit drug use are also low among Asian and Pacific Americans. According to recent data, methamphetamine is the drug most often used by this group.

Treatment is often effective when it involves the family, as many Asian and Pacific-American cultures have values that place greater importance on the influence of extended family members. Acculturation stress and its relationship to substance use should be assessed in recent immigrants. The women of this special population often assume the role of the primary caretaker, and sometimes bear a disproportionate amount of the work of supporting and nurturing children.

Assessment, Clinical Evaluation, Treatment Planning, Family and Community Education and Case Management
(70 hours)

Assessment of Substance Abuse, Lethality, and Levels of Care

Understanding the nature and extent of a client's substance use disorder and how this interacts with other life areas is important for the assessment, diagnosis, case management, and successful treatment. This understanding starts during the assessment and screening process, which allows the counselor to make appropriate plans for treatment services. To ensure the right information is obtained, counselors need to use standardized assessment and screening tools and instruments and follow interview protocols.

Six Areas of Assessment

- Determine client behaviors, values, and frequency of use.

- Identify why substance use is a problem.

- Determine how that patient's life is affected by the substance use.

- Identify the location, timeframe, and method of treatment.

- Recognize any reinforcement for change needed by the patient.

- Examine factors specific to culture and spirituality-related issues.

How Screening and Assessment Differ

Screening is a process of evaluating the presence of a certain problem, and is a process of defining the nature of the problem, deciding on a diagnosis, and creating an appropriate therapy plan. Screening determines whether the substance user needs assessment. The purpose of assessment is to obtain detailed information so the counselor can make a treatment plan.

Factors that Influence Screening and Assessment

Culture and Ethnicity

People from diverse ethnic groups may find the screening and assessment process threatening, foreign, and intrusive. Some cultures have little experience with the American mental health system, so they do not understand questions or the purpose of counseling. Others may have had negative experiences with human service representatives or other treatment programs. An understanding of the cultural basis of the person's beliefs, illness behaviors, and attitudes will provide the counselor with a foundation for developing an appropriate treatment program. Strategies include:

- Instruments and tools should adapted for people of specific cultural groups and populations.

- Interviews conducted in the client's language by a trained staff member.

- Thorough discussion to facilitate full understanding of substance use.

Socioeconomic Status

Counselors should be aware of the expectations as they are based on socioeconomic status. Perceptions could lead to failures to detect drug use in certain patient populations. For instance, healthcare providers often forget to ask middle to upper level income patients about substance use.

Substance Abuse Screening Tools

The objective of substance abuse screening is to identify persons likely to have alcohol or drug use problems. Screening is often conducted by an interview or a short, written questionnaire. Self-administered tools are more likely than face-to-face interviews to elicit honest answers, especially regarding the use of drugs and alcohol. Tools include:

- *The Alcohol Use Disorder Identification Test (AUDIT)* - This is a widely used screening tool effective for identifying heavy drinking. It is a ten-question, self-administered test.

- *The Texas Christian University Drug Screen II (TCUDS II)* - This is a fifteen-item, self-administered substance abuse test that takes around ten minutes to complete. It is widely used in the criminal justice setting.

- *CAGE-AID - The CAGE and CAGE-AID* are questionnaires involving simple tests that screen drug and alcohol consumption.

- *Mini-International Neuropsychiatric Interview (MINI)* - This is a brief, structured interview used for major substance use disorders. It takes around 30 minutes.

Substance Use Assessment

The assessment of a client's life examines details for accurate diagnosis and an appropriate therapy plan and treatment goals. Qualified and trained counselors will perform a comprehensive assessment to determine these things. The assessment should involve multiple avenues to obtain the needed clinical information, such as clinical records, structured interviews, assessment measures, and collateral information. Assessment is a fluid process that continues throughout treatment. Periodic reassessment is necessary for determining client progress and changing therapy needs.

The Assessment Interview

The counselor has to conduct a clinical assessment interview, which requires sensitivity and a considerable amount of time. This is the start of the therapeutic relationship for the client and the counselor. The interviewer should initially explain the reason for the psychosocial history. In addition, the counselor needs to make appropriate referrals within and outside the facility during this time. During the interview, the counselor should:

- Determine the goals of the assessment process.

- Decide what resources are needed to administer and score the assessment instrument, interpret the results, and establish appropriate services.

- Decide what screening measures are required for this client.

- Use a standardized formal assessment tool that offers uniformity and consistency.

The Psychosocial History

This part of the assessment includes:

- *Medical History and Physical Health*: Review HIV/AIDS status, history of hepatitis or other infectious diseases, and HIV/AIDS risk behavior; explore history of gynecological problems, use of birth control and hormone replacement therapy, and the relationship between gynecological problems and substance abuse; obtain history of pregnancies, miscarriages, abortions, and substance abuse during pregnancy; assess need for prenatal care.

- *Substance Abuse History*: Identify people introduced to alcohol and drugs; explore reasons for initiation and continued use; discuss family of origin history of substance abuse, history of use in previous and present significant relationships, and history of use with family members or significant others.

- *Mental Health and Treatment History*: Explore prior treatment history and relationships with prior treatment providers and consequences, if any, for engaging in prior treatment; review history of prior traumatic events, mood or anxiety disorders (including PTSD), as well as eating disorders. Evaluate safety issues including para-suicidal behaviors, previous or current threats, history of interpersonal violence or sexual abuse, and overall feeling of safety. Review family history of mental illness and discuss evidence and history of personal strengths and coping strategies and styles.

- *Interpersonal and Family History*: Obtain history of substance abuse in current relationship, explore acceptance of client's problem among family and significant relationships, discuss concerns regarding child care needs, and discuss the types of support received from family and/or significant other for entering treatment and abstaining from substances.

- *Family, Parenting, and Caregiver History*: Discuss various caregiver roles, review parenting history and current living circumstances.

- *Children's Developmental and Educational History* (applicable to women and children programs): Assess child safety issues and explore developmental, emotional, and medical needs of children.

- *Sociocultural History*: Evaluate client's social support system, including the level of acceptance of her recovery, and discuss level of social isolation prior to treatment. Discuss the role of cultural beliefs pertaining to substance use and recovery process, explore specific cultural attitudes toward women and substance abuse, review current spiritual practices (if any), discuss current acculturation conflicts and stressors and explore need or preference for bilingual or monolingual non-English services.

- *Vocational, Educational, and Military History*: If employed, discuss the level of support that the client is receiving from her employer. Review military history, then expand questions to include history of traumatic events and violence during employment and history of substance abuse in the military; assess financial self-reliance.

- *Legal History*: Discuss history of custody and current involvement with child protective services, if any. Obtain a history of restraining orders, arrests, or periods of incarceration, if any, and determine history of child placement with women who acknowledge past or current incarceration.

- *Barriers to Treatment and Related Services*: Explore financial, housing, health insurance, child care, case management, and transportation needs, and discuss other potential obstacles the client foresees.

- *Strengths and Coping Strategies*: Discuss the challenges that the client has faced throughout her life and how she has managed them, review prior attempts to quit substance use and identify strategies that did work at the time and identify other successes in making changes in other areas of her life.

Assessment Tools for Substance Use Disorders

- *Addiction Severity Index (ASI)* - The most widely used assessment tool. It assesses seven domains of the client's life. The ASI-F is an expanded version that has items added relevant to social, family, and psychiatric aspects.

- *Texas Christian University Brief Intake* - Used to assess drug, alcohol, psychological, legal, medical, and family aspects of the client's life.

- *Drinker Inventory of Consequences (DrinC)* - This tool is self-administered and assesses the negative consequences of drinking in five domains.

- *The Religious Practice and Beliefs Measurement* - A self-assessment tool that reviews religious practices and beliefs.

- *The Multidimensional Measure of Spirituality* - This assessment tool examines domains of spiritual activity, such as values and beliefs.

These are the processes through which counselor, client and available significant others determine the most appropriate initial course of action, given the client's needs and characteristics, and the available resources within the community.

Clinical Screening

Screening establishes rapport and provides a framework for the management of crises, as well as determining need for additional professional assistance.

Knowledge

- Importance and purpose of rapport building.

- Rapport-building methods and issues.

- The range of human emotions and feelings.

- What constitutes a crisis.

- Steps in crisis management.

- Situations in which additional professional assistance may be necessary.

- Available sources of assistance.

- Validated screening instruments, including their purpose, application, and limitations.

- Concepts of reliability and validity as they apply to screening instruments.

- How to interpret the results of screening.

- How to gather and use information from collateral sources.

- How age, developmental level, culture, and gender effect patterns and history of use.

- How age, developmental level, culture, and gender effect communication.

- Client mental status and presenting features, relationship to substance abuse, and psychiatric disorders.

- How to apply confidentiality regulations.

- Symptoms of intoxication, withdrawal, and toxicity for all psychoactive substances, alone and in interaction with one another.

- Physical, pharmacological, and psychological implications of psychoactive substance use.

- Effects of chronic psychoactive substance use or intoxication on cognitive abilities.

- Available resources for help with drug reactions, withdrawal, and violent behavior.

- When to refer for toxicity screening or additional professional help.

- Basic concepts of toxicity screening options, limitations, and legal implications.

- Toxicology reporting language and the meaning of toxicology reports.

- Relationship between psychoactive substance use and violence.

- Basic diagnostic criteria for suicide risk, danger to others, withdrawal syndromes, and major psychiatric disorders.

- Mental and physical conditions that mimic drug intoxication, toxicity, and withdrawal.

- Legal requirements concerning suicide and violence potential.

- Current validated instruments for assessing readiness to change.

- Treatment options.

- Stages of readiness.

- Stages of change models.

- The role of family and significant others in supporting or hindering change.

- The continuum of care and the available range of treatment modalities.

- Current DSM or other accepted criteria for substance use disorders, including strengths, and limitations of such criteria.

- Use of commonly accepted criteria for client placement into levels of care.

- Multi-axis diagnostic criteria.

- Appropriate content and format of the initial action plan.

- Client needs and preferences.

- Available resources for admission or referral.

- Admission and referral protocols.

- Resources for referral.
- Ethical standards regarding referrals.
- Appropriate documentation.
- How to apply confidentiality regulations.

Skills

- Demonstrating effective verbal and nonverbal communication.
- Accurately identifying client's frame of reference.
- Reflecting client's feelings and message.
- Recognizing and defusing volatile or dangerous situations.
- Demonstrating empathy, respect, and genuineness.
- Administering and scoring screening instruments.
- Screening for physical and mental health status.
- Gathering information and collecting data.
- Communicating appropriately.
- Writing accurately, concisely, and legibly.
- Eliciting relevant information from the client.
- Intervening appropriately with a client who may be intoxicated.
- Assessing suicide and/or violence potential.
- Managing crises.
- Attitudes
- Willingness to be respectful toward the client in his or her presenting state.
- Appreciation of the importance of empathy in the face of feelings of anger, hopelessness, suicidal or violent thoughts, and feelings.
- Appreciation of the importance of legal obligations.
- Assist the client in identifying the impact of substance use on his or her current life problems and the effects of continued harmful use or abuse. Knowledge
- The progression and characteristics of substance use disorders.

- The effects of psychoactive substances on behavior, thinking, feelings, health status, and relationships.

- Denial and other defense mechanisms in client resistance.

- Establishing a therapeutic relationship.

- Demonstrating effective communication skills.

- Determining and confirming the effects of substance use on life problems with the client.

- Assessing client readiness to address substance use issues.

- Interpreting the client's perception of his or her experiences.

- Attitudes

- Respect for the client's perception of his or her experiences.

- Determine the client's readiness for treatment and change as well as the needs of others involved in the current situation.

- Eliciting and determining relevant client characteristics, needs, and goals.

- Making appropriate recommendations for treatment.

- Attitudes

- Recognition of one's own treatment biases.

- Appreciation of various treatment approaches.

- Apply accepted criteria for diagnosis of substance use disorders in making treatment recommendations.

- Using current DSM or other accepted diagnostic standards.

- Using appropriate placement criteria.

- Obtaining information necessary to develop a diagnostic impression. Attitudes

- Recognition of personal and professional limitations of practice, based on knowledge and training.

- Willingness to base treatment recommendations on the client's best interest.

- Construct with client and appropriate others an initial action plan based on client needs, preferences, and resources available.

- Developing the action plan in collaboration with the client and appropriate others.

- Documenting the action plan.

- Contracting with the client concerning initial action plan.

- Communicating clearly and appropriately.

- Networking and advocating with service providers.

- Negotiating and advocating client admissions to appropriate treatment resources.

- Facilitating client follow-through.

- Documenting accurately and appropriately.

Attitudes

- Recognition of personal biases, values, and beliefs, and their effect on communication and the treatment process.

- Willingness to establish rapport.

- Gather data systematically from the client and other available collateral sources, using screening instruments and other methods that are sensitive to age, developmental level, culture, and gender. At a minimum, data should include current and historic substance use; health, mental health, and substance related treatment history; mental status; and current social, environmental, and/or economic constraints.

- Appreciation of the value of the data gathering process.

- Willingness to work collaboratively with clients and others.

- Based on initial action plan, take specific steps to initiate an admission or referral and ensure follow-through.

- Willingness to renegotiate.

Clinical Assessment

The assessment is an ongoing process through which the counselor collaborates with the client and others to gather and interpret information necessary for planning treatment and evaluating client progress. During this process, the counselor must select and use a comprehensive assessment process that is sensitive to age, gender, racial and ethnic cultural issues, and disabilities that includes, but is not limited to:

- History of alcohol and other drug use
- Physical health, mental health, and addiction treatment history
- Family issues
- Work history and career issues
- History of criminality
- Psychological, emotional, and world-view concerns
- Current status of physical health, mental health, and substance use
- Spirituality
- Education and basic life skills
- Socio-economic characteristics, lifestyle, and current legal status
- Use of community resources.
- Knowledge
- Basic concepts of test validity and reliability.
- Current validated assessment instruments and their subscales.
- Appropriate use and limitations of standardized instruments.
- The range of life areas to be assessed
- How age, developmental level, racial and ethnic culture, gender, and disabilities can influence the validity and appropriateness of assessment instruments.

Knowledge

- Appropriate scoring methodology.
- How to analyze and interpret results.
- The range of available treatment options
- The counselor's role, responsibilities, and scope of practice.
- The limits of the counselor's training and education.
- The supervisor's role.
- Available consultation services and roles of consultants.
- The multidisciplinary assessment approach.

- Agency-specific protocols and procedures.
- Appropriate terminology and abbreviations.
- Legal implications of actions and documentation.
- How to apply confidentiality regulations.

Skills

- Selecting and administering appropriate assessment instruments within the counselor's scope of practice.
- Introducing and explaining the purpose of assessment.
- Addressing client perceptions and providing appropriate explanations of instrument items.
- Conducting comprehensive assessment interviews and collecting information from collateral sources.
- Scoring assessment tools.
- Interpreting data relevant to the client.
- Using results to identify appropriate treatment options.
- Communicating recommendations to the client and other appropriate service providers.
- Recognizing the need for assistance from a supervisor.
- Recognizing when consultation is appropriate.
- Providing appropriate documentation.
- Communicating information clearly.
- Incorporating information from supervision and consultation into assessment findings.
- Providing clear, concise, and legible documentation.
- Incorporating information from various sources.
- Preparing and presenting oral and written assessment findings to the client and other professionals within the bounds of how to apply confidentiality regulations.

Attitudes

- Respect for the limits of assessment instruments and one's ability to interpret them.

- Analyze and interpret the data to determine treatment recommendations

- Respect for the value of assessment in determining appropriate treatment.

- Seek appropriate supervision and consultation.

- Commitment to professionalism.

- Acceptance of one's own personal and professional limitations.

- Document assessment findings and treatment recommendations.

- Recognition of the value of accurate documentation.

A patient's person-centered change plan must take into consideration special circumstances such as cultural, sexual, and spiritual beliefs. Part of this process is to detect issues and developmental delays that occur due to a lack of life skill techniques.

For effective person-centered treatment, the counselor should involve family if possible, as well as identify an alternate plan. Experts who study the process of recovery from addiction have determined that family involvement is an important part of the recovery process, so it should be implemented whenever possible. Person-centered therapy has shown to be most effective when the counselor involves the family in both the assessment and planning process of the treatment and recovery.

Another aspect of person-centered treatment involves providing educational processes that revolve around continued recovery. To do this, the counselor can use groups for peer support. Lack of proper support is often present with addicts, so providing users with peers that they can rely on will help them through the process of recovery by relating to others.

For person-centered therapy, the counselor should use caution when discussing any type of medication with the patient who is in recovery. The patient must also be educated on use and harm-reduction techniques that they can use to help reduce harm to themselves and reduce their amount of use.

An important aspect of person-centered treatment involves arranging care with a case manager. During treatment, the case manager helps the patient to develop the skills needed to find employment and survive independently without drugs once the treatment program is over. The case manager should ensure that the plan created between the counselor and the patient is sensitive to the patient's individual needs.

Co-Occurring Mental Disorders

When both substance abuse and a mental disorder are present, the plan created for the patient's treatment must be unique. It is considered to be a "dual diagnosis" by medical professionals. By implementing the proper treatment plan for co-occurring mental disorders, the process of recovery will be much easier for the individual and that person will have a much greater chances of success.

Mental illness could cause the patient to resist treatment approaches. Depending on the type of mental disorder present, the patient may think of the treatment center as a negative place, leading to withdrawal and relapse.

Issues Regarding Dual Approach

Part of the counselor's job when dealing with co-occurring mental disorders is recognizing that both issues need to be addressed during the treatment process. By addressing only substance use, true mental health issues can be overlooked and can trigger the substance use to come back. By addressing both issues at once, the probability of recovery from drugs and alcohol abuse increases greatly.

To assist a patient with co-occurring mental disorders, the counselor must work to help the patient to find a group with these common issues. For example, those suffering from depression may be able to better relate with the group that offers support for patients with both depression and substance abuse issues.

The counselor should have a psychiatric medication administered to the patient when applicable, after a psychiatric evaluation by a medical professional. The medication may help the cravings of the substance addiction, as it works to address both issues.

Configuration Styles

- Gentle approach - A less forceful approach to recovery may offer better results for some patients.

- Multiple intervention approach - Use of multiple intervention techniques will help when the patient is reluctant to accept their mental disorder.

- Unique approach - When substance abuse and a mental disorder is present, a unique treatment plan must be used for the patient. The method used is unique when compared to the process of treatment for someone with only an addiction problem.

Case managers and counselors are two separate types of support for the patient recovering from addiction. By incorporating case management and counselor techniques, a single entry of progression regarding the patient is incorporated. Lack of proper incorporation of case management and counseling techniques can create barriers between systems that could affect the recovery process for the patient, a lack of agreement on a plan, and a lack of infinitives for progression.

Treatment Models

There are different models involved in the treatment process, which involve using both case management and counselor techniques in order to provide proper patient care. These models provide effective treatment, and the different approaches used help the patient in all areas of life.

Assertive Community Therapy Model
Assertive community therapy provides a wide range of therapy services and helps to implement the services into the patient's everyday life. This therapy includes job assistance, skills building, and other valuable resources. The assertive community therapy model:

- Has seven areas of emphasis.

- Creates a natural setting for client care. For example, the care may be provided in home for the patient or in a familiar environment.

- Focuses on activities of daily living.

- Creates asserted advocacy.

- Involves continuous and frequent client contact between the case managers and the counselor.

- Involves shared cases that use team products.

- Creates long-term communication between the case manager and the counselor during the patient's treatment process.

- Focuses on mental health as well as addresses substance abuse treatment options.

Broker Generalist Model

The most basic type of case management, the broker generalist model allows the case manager to detect problems and provide necessary services. It is considered the most effective model when treatment providers and social service workers require additional information regarding the patient.

Process Treatment Model

This is the treatment model where the patient agrees for treatment when they reach bottom rather than when being forced into treatment. This model allows the patient what he or she needs in order to progress in the transition with proper support. It also focuses on patient strengths and expands upon them by encouraging and developing a helping network, creating a strong case management and client relationship, and providing active and aggressive care for the patient at all times.

Strategy-Based Model

The strategy-based model involves a process when a patient who has a mental illness transfers from an inpatient or outpatient facility. The counselor must offer support by providing resources to the client in terms of housing, employment, and social support resources. This model is designed to help clients use their own strengths as a tool to acquire the resources they need in order to have a successful recovery.

Clinical Rehabilitation Therapy Model

Clinical rehabilitation therapy joins clinical treatment with case management. The case manager addresses issues regarding client services, which can include life skills, psychotherapy, and family therapy. Both types of treatment can be used on their own and combined together to gain optimal results and determine the progression of the patient. The clinical rehabilitation therapy model is a combined approach, and thought to be an effective strategy for patients with co-occurring mental disorders.

Case Management Model

Applied to help patients see and address issues that they may have, the case management model helps develop a motor for change in the patient's new skills, which is used to implement the necessary change. Once a plan for change is designed by the case manager, the patient is encouraged to apply these techniques to daily life. Engagement encourages the patient to reach out for help when necessary.

Case Management Techniques

Case management techniques, which should be applied during pre-treatment, include:

- Providing resources to the patient that not only help with the transition but also help the person to live a better life. For example, developing and maintaining social relationships.

- Properly addressing issues during treatment process

- Offering safe housing and addressing substance abuse issues during the pretreatment phase.

- Addressing issues such as anger, lack of understanding, and mental health service denial. This will ensure that recovery is more successful when the patient enters the treatment phase.

- Detecting and addressing problems not previously addressed. For example, a minimalist may act as if there is no problem with their substance use, which will make treatment ineffective.

- Detecting issues such as missed appointments, continued substance use, multiple excuses, no commitment to recovery, and apathy.

Primary Treatment

Primary treatment techniques aim to help the patient make a delicate transition in all areas of the treatment process together. This is done prior to leaving the inpatient program. Primary treatment addresses the aftercare needs of the patient during the primary phase of therapy. For example, housing needs, follow-up treatment program issues, support systems, financial needs, and health issues all are things that will need to be addressed for aftercare.

With primary treatment, the counselor must address the dental and medical needs of the patient. Often, dental and medical care is offered for the first time in years during primary treatment, so proper monitoring of the medication should be done at all times. Counselors and case managers must work as advocates during health treatment for the patient.

The Primary Treatment Assessment Process

The focus of addiction treatment and identification of various patient needs for common services are done during the assessment process. This involves:

- Detecting special skills or defects within the patient.

- Providing basic supplemental needs to the patient.

- Identifying the level of regular ability to function with the patient.

- Detecting various patient risk strategies.

Primary Treatment Results

Treatment results are generated by the patient with the help of the counselor and/or case manager. Treatment can be effective when:

- An effective service plan is created.

- Treatment occurs in a forward motion during the recovery phases.

- Support is provided when transitioning from the inpatient and outpatient program.

- Issues are addressed while using residential treatment program.

- Both the patient and the counselor start the treatment program through the use of primary treatment.

Primary Treatment Goals

Goals for primary treatment are created between the patient and case manager. In order to make both long- and short-term goals, the counselor must:

- Offer continued motivation to the patient in order to engage in positive progression in the treatment process.
- Determine the proper timing of application of service to get appropriate treatment.
- Offer support to the patient during the transitional phase.
- Use intervention to avoid crises and respond when appropriate.
- Provide the patient with the skills needed for independence.
- Create an external support structure to facilitate independence, and use community integration.

Primary Treatment Techniques

The techniques used by the counselor serve to reduce both external and internal patient barriers. The plan created must be used directly after the assessment process. When used with the patient, this plan includes:

- Planning for proper treatment.
- Setting goals.
- Implementing the goals. This is most effective when broken up into smaller goals by creating objectives, outlining steps, and determining the objects of goals.

Lack of meeting a goal allows the patient the chance to assess the situation and then reevaluate the steps they are taking to meet the goal as well as what needs to be changed in order to make it achievable. A careful approach to implementation of the steps offers the patient with resources to go beyond the basic needs.

Treatment Planning

Treatment is a collaborative process through which the counselor and client develop desired treatment outcomes and identify the strategies for achieving them. At a minimum, the treatment plan addresses the identified substance use disorder(s), as well as issues related to treatment progress, including relationships with family and significant others, employment, education, spirituality, health concerns, and legal needs. Additionally, treatment involves obtaining and interpreting all relevant assessment information.

Knowledge

- Stages of change and readiness for treatment.
- The treatment planning process.
- Motivation and motivating factors.
- The role and importance of client resources and barriers to treatment.
- The impact that the client and family systems have on treatment decisions and outcomes.
- Other sources of assessment information.
- How to apply confidentiality regulations.
- Effective communication styles.
- Factors affecting the client's comprehension of assessment findings.
- Roles and expectations of others potentially involved in treatment.
- Effective communication styles.
- Methods to elicit feedback.
- Available treatment modalities, client placement criteria, and cost issues.
- The effectiveness of the various treatment models based on current research.
- Implications of various treatment alternatives, including no treatment.
- Motivational processes.
- Stages of change models.
- Treatment sequencing and the continuum of care.
- Hierarchy of needs.

- Interrelationship among client needs and problems.
- Levels of client motivation.
- Treatment needs of diverse populations.
- How to write measurable outcome statements.
- Intervention strategies.
- Level of client's interest in making specific changes.
- Treatment issues with diverse populations.
- Treatment modalities and community resources.
- Contributions of other professions and mutual-help or self-help support groups.
- Current placement criteria.
- The importance of client's racial or ethnic culture, age, developmental level, gender, and life circumstances in coordinating resources to client needs.
- The relationship among problem statements, desired outcomes, and treatment strategies.
- Short- and long-term treatment planning.
- Evaluation methodology.
- Federal, State, and agency confidentiality regulations, requirements, and policies.
- Resources for legal consultation.
- Effective communication styles.
- How to evaluate treatment and stages of recovery.
- When and how to review and revise the treatment plan.

Skills

- Establishing treatment priorities based on all available data.
- Working with clients of different age, developmental levels, gender, racial, and ethnic cultures.
- Interpreting data.
- Translating assessment information into treatment goal and outcomes.

- Summarizing and synthesizing assessment results.
- Assessing client for understanding and correcting misunderstandings.
- Communicating with clients in a manner that is sensitive to cultural and gender issues.
- Communicating assessment findings to interested parties within the bounds of confidentiality regulations and practice standards.
- Eliciting feedback.
- Working collaboratively.
- Establishing trusting relationship.
- Synthesizing available data to establish treatment priorities.
- Explaining the treatment process.
- Presenting information in a non-judgmental manner.
- Selecting treatment settings appropriate for client needs and preferences.
- Building partnerships with client and significant others.
- Assessing and developing strategies to overcome barriers.
- Eliciting the client's preferences for treatment.
- Promoting the client's readiness to accept treatment.
- Timing, sequencing, and prioritizing.
- Translating assessment information into measurable treatment goals and outcome statements.
- Working with the client to develop realistic time frames for completing goals.
- Engaging, contracting, and negotiating with the client.
- Identifying alternate approaches tailored to client needs.
- Implementing strategies in terms understandable to the client.
- Coordinating resources and solutions with client needs, desires, and preferences.
- Explaining the rationale behind treatment recommendations.
- Summarizing mutually agreed upon recommendations.
- Individualizing treatment plans that balance strengths and resources with problems and deficits.

- Negotiating.
- Collaborating and contracting with the client in developing an action plan in positive, proactive terms.
- Establishing criteria to evaluate progress.
- Communicating the roles of various interested parties and support systems.
- Explaining client rights and responsibilities and applicable regulations regarding confidentiality.
- Responding to questions and providing clarification as needed.
- Referring to appropriate legal authority.
- Modifying the treatment plan based on review of client progress and/or changing circumstances.
- Problem solving.
- Engaging, negotiating, and contracting.
- Eliciting client feedback on treatment experiences.

Attitudes

- Appreciation of the strengths and limitations of the client and significant others.
- Recognition of the value of thoroughness and follow-through.
- Explain assessment findings to the client and significant others involved in potential treatment.
- Recognition of one's own treatment biases.
- Willingness to consider multiple approaches to recovery and change.
- Recognition of the client's right and need to understand assessment results.
- Respect for the roles of others.
- Provide the client and significant others with clarification and further information as needed.
- Willingness to communicate interactively with the client and significant others.
- Examine treatment implications in collaboration with the client and significant others.

- Willingness to negotiate with the client.

- Open-mindedness toward a variety of approaches.

- Respect for input from client and significant others.

- Confirm the readiness of the client and significant others to participate in treatment.

- Respect for client values and goals.

- Patience and perseverance.

- Prioritize client needs in the order they will be addressed.

- Sensitivity to the client's needs and perceptions.

- Formulate mutually agreed upon and measurable treatment outcome statements for each need.

- Respect for the client's treatment and life goals.

- Respect for the client's individual pace toward change.

- Appreciation for incremental treatment goals and achievements.

- Identify appropriate strategies for each outcome.

- Respect for client and others.

- Appreciation for various treatment strategies.

- Coordinate treatment activities and community resources with prioritized client needs in a manner consistent with the client's diagnosis and existing placement criteria.

- Acceptance of a variety of treatment approaches.

- Recognition of the importance of coordinating treatment activities.

- Develop with the client a mutually acceptable plan of action and method for monitoring and evaluating progress.

- Sensitivity to gender and cultural issues.

- Recognition of the value of monitoring outcome.

- Willingness to negotiate.

- Inform client of confidentiality rights, program procedures that safeguard them, and the exceptions imposed by regulations.

- Respect for client confidentiality rights.

- Commitment to professionalism.

- Recognition of the importance of professional collaboration within the bounds of confidentiality.

- Reassess the treatment plan at regular intervals and/or when indicated by changing circumstances.

- Recognition of the value of client input into treatment goals and process.

- Openness when critically examining one's own work.

- Receptivity to client feedback.

- Willingness to learn from clinical supervision and modify practice appropriately.

Counselors are at high risk for burnout when caring for recovering addicts. People with substance abuse issues and those with mental health disorders often are of low socioeconomic statuses, require much assistance, and can be quite demanding. Taking self-care actions is critical for a counselor's success in this field. These include:

- Recognizing negative thought patterns. This is important because negative thoughts can slow down or alter the process of treatment for the patient.

- Recognizing these emotions allows the counselor to identify personal reactions and change thoughts by practicing coping techniques for stress and negative thinking.

- The counselor must continue examination of these negative thought patterns each time they occur in a negative manner in order to achieve the highest level of results.

Self-Care and Stress Reduction
- Consider a view of various certification components and sign a timeframe to achieve different components.

- Make your goals realistic.

- Examine various stages of stress and determine the cause of the stress.

- Memorize a positive statement and make progress.

- Don't aim for perfection. Regard your effort more than the outcome.

- Use the "one step at a time" strategy.

- Care for your mind by relaxing during stressful times.

- Care for your body by spending time with a supportive circle and expressing your emotions.

- Care for your spirit by learning to forgive yourself during times of failure and implementing positive thinking during this time.

- Utilize resources available within the community to help prevent negative consequences due to overexertion. For example, negative emotions and burnout are related to overexertion and can be worked upon with in the professional community with those who offer support.

Community-Based Stress Prevention

To help a client deal with stress, the counselor can use community-based stress prevention. These prevention tactics include:

- Developing a strong support system within the community, particularly with people with similar beliefs as yours. Within the group, your behaviors tend to become similar to the behaviors of others.

- Create a group outside of the mental health system for support

Benefits of Community-Based Support

Community-based principles have shown to be effective, including benefits provided by:

- Compassion
- Commitment
- Involvement
- Leadership
- Communication affect
- Problem-solving

Referral

A referral is the process of facilitating the client's utilization of available support systems and community resources to meet needs identified in clinical evaluation and/or treatment planning. Referrals establish and maintain relations with civic groups, agencies, other professionals, governmental entities, and the community-at-large to ensure appropriate referrals, identify service gaps, expand community resources, and help to address unmet needs.

The counselor must have an understanding of the mission, function, resources, and quality of services offered by many community based organizations. These include: civic groups, community groups, and neighborhood organizations; religious organizations; governmental entities; health and allied health care systems (managed care); criminal justice systems; housing administrations; employment and vocational rehabilitation services; child care facilities; crisis intervention programs; abused persons programs; mutual and self-help groups; cultural enhancement organizations; advocacy groups; and other agencies.

Knowledge

- Community demographics.

- The community's political and cultural systems.

- Criteria for receiving community services, including fee and funding structures.

- How to access community agencies and service providers.

- State and Federal legislative mandates and regulations.

- Confidentiality regulations.

- Service gaps and appropriate ways of advocating for new resources.

- Effective communication styles.

- The needs of the client population served.

- How to access current information on the function, mission, and resources of community service providers.

- How to access current information on referral criteria and accreditation status of community service providers.

- How to access client satisfaction data regarding community service providers.

- Client motivation and ability to initiate and follow through with referrals.

- Factors in determining the optimal time to engage client in referral process.

- Clinical assessment methods.

- Empowerment techniques.

- Crisis intervention methods.

- Comprehensive treatment planning.

- Methods of assessing client's progress toward treatment goals.

- How to tailor resources to client treatment needs.

- How to access key resource persons in community service provider network.

- Mission, function, and resources of appropriate community service providers.

- Referral protocols of selected service providers.

- Logistics necessary for client access and follow through with the referral.

- Applicable confidentiality regulations and protocols.

- Factors to consider when determining the appropriate time to engage client in referral process.

- How treatment planning and referral relate to the goals of recovery.

- How client defenses, abilities, personal preferences, cultural influences, presentation, and appearance affect referral and follow through.

- Comprehensive referral information and protocols.

- Terminology and structure used in referral settings.

- Mission, function, and resources of the referral agency or professional.

- Protocols and documentation necessary to make referral.

- Pertinent local, State, and Federal confidentiality regulations, applicable client rights and responsibilities, client consent procedures, and other guiding principles for exchange of relevant information.

- Ethical standards of practice related to this exchange of information

- Methods of assessing client's progress toward treatment goals.

- Appropriate sources and techniques for evaluating referral outcomes.

Skills

- Networking and communication.
- Using existing community resource directories including computer databases.
- Advocating for clients.
- Working with others as part of a team.
- Establishing and nurturing collaborative relationships with key contacts in community service organizations.
- Interpreting and using evaluation and client feedback data.
- Giving feedback to community resources regarding their service delivery
- Interpreting assessment and treatment planning materials to determine appropriateness of client or counselor referral.
- Assessing the client's readiness to participate in the referral process.
- Educating the client regarding appropriate referral processes.
- Motivating clients to take responsibility for referral and follow-up.
- Applying crisis intervention techniques.
- Using written and verbal communication for successful referrals.
- Using appropriate technology to access, collect, and forward necessary documentation.
- Conforming to all applicable confidentiality regulations and protocols.
- Documenting the referral process accurately.
- Maintaining and nurturing relationships with key contacts in community.
- Maintaining follow-up activity with client.
- Using language and terms the client will easily understand.
- Interpreting the treatment plan and how referral relates to progress.
- Engaging in effective communication related to the referral process: - negotiating, - educating, - personalizing risks and benefits, - contracting.
- Using written and verbal communication for successful referrals.
- Using appropriate technology to access, collect, and forward relevant information needed by the agency or professional.
- Obtaining informed client consent and documentation needed for the

exchange of relevant information.

- Reporting relevant information accurately and objectively.
- Using appropriate measurement processes and instruments.
- Collecting objective and subjective data on the referral process.

Attitudes

- Respect for interdisciplinary service delivery.
- Respect for both client needs and agency services.
- Respect for collaboration and cooperation.
- Patience and perseverance.
- Continuously assess and evaluate referral resources to determine their appropriateness.
- Respect for confidentiality regulations.
- Willingness to advocate on behalf of the client.
- Differentiate between situations in which it is most appropriate for the client to self-refer to a resource and instances requiring counselor referral.
- Respect for the client's ability to initiate and follow-up with referral.
- Willingness to share decision-making power with the client.
- Respect for the goal of positive self-determination.
- Recognition of the counselor's responsibility to carry out client advocacy when needed.
- Arrange referrals to other professionals, agencies, community programs, or other appropriate resources to meet client needs.
- Respect for the client and the client's needs.
- Respect for collaboration and cooperation.
- Respect for interdisciplinary, comprehensive approaches to meet client needs.
- Explain in clear and specific language the necessity for and process of referral to increase the likelihood of client understanding and follow through.
- Awareness of personal biases toward referral resources.

- Exchange relevant information with the agency or professional to whom the referral is being made in a manner consistent with confidentiality regulations and generally accepted professional standards of care.

- Commitment to professionalism.

- Respect for the importance of confidentiality regulations and professional standards.

- Appreciation for the need to exchange relevant information with other professionals.

- Evaluate the outcome of the referral.

- Appreciation of the value of the evaluation process.

- Appreciation of the value of inter-agency collaboration.

- Appreciation of the value of interdisciplinary referral.

Service Coordination

Service coordination involves the administrative, clinical, and evaluative activities that bring the client, treatment services, community agencies, and other resources together to focus on issues and needs identified in the treatment plan. Service coordination, which includes case management and client advocacy, establishes a framework of action for the client to achieve specified goals. It involves collaboration with the client and significant others, coordination of treatment and referral services, liaison activities with community resources and managed care systems, client advocacy, and ongoing evaluation of treatment progress and client needs. To implement a treatment plan, you must initiate collaboration with a referral source.

Knowledge

- How to access and transmit information necessary for referral.

- Missions, functions, and resources of community service network.

- Managed care and other systems affecting the client.

- Eligibility criteria for referral to community service providers.

- Appropriate confidentiality regulations.

- Terminologies appropriate to the referral source.

- Methods for obtaining relevant screening, assessment, and initial treatment-planning information.
- How to interpret information for the purpose of service coordination.
- Theory, concepts, and philosophies of screening and assessment tools.
- How to define long- and short-term goals of treatment.
- Biopsychosocial assessment methods.
- Philosophies, policies, procedures, and admission protocols for community agencies.
- Eligibility criteria for referral to community service providers.
- Principles for tailoring treatment to client needs.
- Methods of assessing and documenting client change over time.
- Federal and State confidentiality regulations.
- Admission criteria and protocols.
- Documentation requirements and confidentiality regulations.
- Appropriate Federal, State, and local regulations related to admission.
- Funding mechanisms, reimbursement protocols, and required documentation.
- Protocols required by managed care organizations.
- Functions and resources provided by treatment services and managed care systems.
- Available community services.
- Effective communication styles.
- Client rights and responsibilities.
- Treatment schedule, time frames, discharge criteria, and costs.
- Rules and regulations of the treatment program.
- Role and limitations of significant others in treatment.
- How to apply confidentiality regulations.
- Methods for determining the client's treatment status.
- Documenting and reporting methods used by community agencies.
- Service reimbursement issues and their impact on the treatment plan.

- Case presentation techniques and protocols.
- Applicable confidentiality regulations.
- Terminology and methods used by community agencies.

Skills

- Using appropriate technology to access, collect, summarize, and transmit referral data on client.
- Communicating respect and empathy for cultural and lifestyle differences.
- Demonstrating appropriate written and verbal communication.
- Establishing trust and rapport with colleagues in the community.
- Assessing level and intensity of client care needed.
- Using accurate, clear, and concise written and verbal communication.
- Interpreting, prioritizing, and using client information.
- Soliciting comprehensive and accurate information from numerous sources including the client.
- Using appropriate technology to document appropriate information.
- Working with client to select the most appropriate treatment.
- Accessing available funding resources.
- Using effective communication styles.
- Recognizing, documenting, and communicating client change.
- Involving family and significant others in treatment planning.
- Demonstrating accurate, clear, and concise written and verbal communication.
- Using language the client will easily understand.
- Negotiating with diverse treatment systems.
- Advocating for client services.
- Demonstrating clear and concise written and verbal communication.
- Establishing appropriate boundaries with client and significant others.
- Delivering case presentations.

- Using appropriate technology to collect and interpret client treatment information from diverse sources.
- Demonstrating accurate, clear, and concise verbal and written communication.
- Participating in interdisciplinary team building.
- Participating in negotiation, advocacy, conflict-resolution, problem solving, and mediation.

Attitudes

- Respect for contributions and needs of multiple disciplines to treatment process.
- Confidence in using diverse systems and treatment approaches.
- Open-mindedness to a variety of treatment approaches.
- Willingness to modify or adapt plans.
- Obtain, review, and interpret all relevant screening, assessment, and initial treatment-planning information.
- Appreciation for all sources and types of data and their possible treatment implications.
- Awareness of personal biases that may impact work with client.
- Respect for client self-assessment and reporting.
- Confirm the client's eligibility for admission and continued readiness for treatment and change.
- Recognition of the importance of continued support, encouragement, and optimism.
- Willingness to accept the limitations of treatment for some clients.
- Appreciation for the goal of self-determination.
- Recognition of the importance of family and significant others to treatment planning.
- Appreciation of the need for continuing assessment and modifications to the treatment plan.
- Complete necessary administrative procedures for admission to treatment.

- Acceptance of the necessity to deal with bureaucratic systems.

- Recognition of the importance of cooperation.

- Patience and perseverance.

- Establish accurate treatment and recovery expectations with the client and involved significant others including, but not limited to nature of services, program goals, program procedures, rules regarding client conduct, schedule of treatment activities, costs of treatment, factors affecting duration of care, client rights and responsibilities.

- Respect for the contribution of clients and significant others.

- Coordinate all treatment activities with services provided to the client by other resources.

- Willingness to collaborate.

Consulting

Consulting involves summarizing the client's personal and cultural background, treatment plan, recovery progress, and problems inhibiting progress for purposes of assuring quality of care, gaining feedback, and planning changes in the course of treatment.

Knowledge

- Methods for assessing the client's past and present biopsychosocial status.

- Methods for assessing social systems that may affect the client's progress.

- Methods for continuous assessment and modification of the treatment plan.

- Functions and unique terminology of related disciplines.

- Roles, responsibilities, and areas of expertise of other team members and disciplines.

- Confidentiality regulations.

- Team dynamics and group process.

- Federal, State, and local confidentiality regulations.

- How to apply confidentiality regulations to documentation and sharing of client information.

- Ethical standards related to confidentiality.
- Client rights and responsibilities.
- Behaviors appropriate to professional collaboration.
- Client rights and responsibilities.

Skills

- Demonstrating clear and concise written and verbal communication.
- Synthesizing information and developing modified treatment goals and objectives.
- Soliciting and interpreting feedback related to the treatment plan.
- Prioritizing and documenting relevant client data.
- Observing and identifying problems that might impede progress.
- Soliciting client satisfaction feedback.
- Demonstrating accurate, clear, and concise verbal and written communication.
- Participating in interdisciplinary collaboration.
- Interpreting written and verbal data from various sources.
- Demonstrating clear and concise verbal and written communication.
- Participating in problem solving, decision making, mediation, and advocacy.
- Communicating about confidentiality issues.
- Coordinating the client's treatment with representatives of multiple disciplines.
- Participating in team building and group process.
- Explaining and applying confidentiality regulations.
- Obtaining informed consent.
- Communicating with the client, family and significant others, and with other service providers within the boundaries of existing confidentiality regulations.
- Establishing and maintaining non-judgmental, respectful relationships with clients and other service providers.
- Demonstrating clear, concise, accurate communication with other

professionals or agencies.

- Applying confidentiality regulations when communicating with agencies.
- Transferring client information to other service providers in a professional manner.

Attitudes

- Respect for the personal nature of the information shared by the client and significant others.
- Respect for interdisciplinary work.
- Appreciation for incremental changes.
- Recognition of relapse as an opportunity for positive change.
- Understand terminology, procedures, and roles of other disciplines related to the treatment of substance use disorders.
- Comfort in asking questions and providing information across disciplines.
- Contribute as part of a multidisciplinary treatment team.
- Interest in cooperation and collaboration with diverse service providers.
- Respect and appreciation for other team members and their disciplines.
- Apply confidentiality regulations appropriately.
- Recognition of the importance of confidentiality regulations.
- Respect for a client's right to privacy.
- Demonstrate respect and non-judgmental attitudes toward clients in all contacts with community professionals and agencies.
- Willingness to advocate on behalf of the client.
- Professional concern for the client.
- Commitment to professionalism.

Continued Assessment and Planning

Continued assessment and planning involves maintaining ongoing contact with client and involving significant others to ensure adherence to the treatment plan.

Knowledge

- Social, cultural, and family systems.
- Techniques to engage the client in treatment process.
- Outreach, follow-up, and aftercare techniques.
- Methods for determining the client's goals, treatment plan, and motivational level.
- Assessment mechanisms to measure client's progress toward treatment objectives.
- How to recognize incremental progress toward treatment goals.
- Client's cultural norms, biases, unique characteristics, and preferences for treatment.
- Generally accepted treatment outcome measures.
- Methods for evaluating treatment progress.
- Methods for assessing client's motivation and adherence to treatment plans.
- Theories and principles of the stages of change and recovery.
- Continuum of care.
- Interviewing techniques.
- Stages in the treatment and recovery process.
- Individual differences in the recovery process.
- Methods for evaluating treatment progress.
- Methods for re-involving the client in the treatment planning process.
- Treatment modalities.
- Documentation of process, progress, and outcome.
- Factors affecting client's success in treatment.
- Treatment planning.
- Treatment outcome measures.

- Understand concepts of validity and reliability of outcome measures.
- Treatment planning process.
- Continuum of care.
- Available social and family systems for continuing care.
- Available community resources for continuing care.
- Signs and symptoms of relapse.
- Relapse prevention strategies.
- Family and social systems theories.
- Discharge planning process.
- Documentation requirements including, but not limited to: - addiction counseling, - other disciplines, - funding sources, - agencies and service providers.
- Service coordination role in the treatment process.
- Treatment planning along the continuum of care.
- Initial and on-going placement criteria.
- Methods to assess current and on-going client status.
- Stages of progress associated with treatment modalities.
- Appropriate discharge indicators.

Skills

- Engaging client, family, and significant others in the ongoing treatment process.
- Assessing client progress toward treatment goals.
- Helping the client maintain motivation to change.
- Assessing the comprehension level of the client, family, and significant others.
- Documenting the client's adherence to the treatment plan.
- Recognizing and addressing ambivalence and resistance.
- Implementing follow-up and aftercare protocols.
- Identifying and documenting change.

- Assessing adherence to treatment plans.

- Applying treatment outcome measures.

- Communicating with people of other cultures.

- Reinforcing positive change.

- Participating in conflict resolution, problem solving, and mediation.

- Observing, recognizing, assessing, and documenting client progress.

- Eliciting client perspectives on progress.

- Demonstrating clear and concise written and verbal communication.

- Interviewing individuals, groups, and families.

- Acquiring and prioritizing relevant treatment information.

- Assisting the client in maintaining motivation.

- Maintaining contact with client, referral sources, and significant others.

- Demonstrating clear and concise oral and written communication.

- Observing and assessing client progress.

- Engaging client in the treatment process.

- Applying progress and outcome measures.

- Using outcome measures in the treatment planning process.

- Accessing information from referral sources.

- Demonstrating clear and concise oral and written communication.

- Assessing and documenting treatment progress.

- Participating in confrontation, conflict resolution, and problem solving.

- Collaborating with referral sources.

- Engaging client and significant others in treatment process and continuing care.

- Assisting client to develop a relapse prevention plan.

- Demonstrating clear and concise written communication.

- Using appropriate technology to report information in an accurate and timely manner within the bounds of confidentiality regulations.

- Observing and assessing client progress.

- Demonstrating clear and concise written and verbal communication.
- Participating in conflict resolution, problem solving, mediation, and negotiation.
- Tailoring treatment to meet client needs.
- Applying for placement, continued stay, and discharge criteria.

Attitudes

- Professional concern for the client, the family, and significant others.
- Therapeutic optimism.
- Recognition of relapse as an opportunity for positive change.
- Patience and perseverance.
- Understand and recognize stages of change and other signs of treatment progress.
- Appreciation for cultural issues that impact treatment progress.
- Respect for individual differences.
- Therapeutic optimism.
- Assess treatment and recovery progress and, in consultation with the client and significant others, make appropriate changes to the treatment plan to ensure progress toward treatment goals.
- Willingness to be flexible.
- Respect for the client's right to self-determination.
- Appreciation of the role significant others play in the recovery process.
- Appreciation of individual differences in the recovery process.
- Describe and document treatment process, progress, and outcome.
- Appreciation of the importance of accurate documentation.
- Recognition of the importance of multidisciplinary treatment planning.
- Use accepted treatment outcome measures.
- Appreciation of the need to measure outcomes.
- Conduct continuing care, relapse prevention, and discharge planning with the client and involved significant others.

- Therapeutic optimism.

- Patience and perseverance.

- Document service coordination activities throughout the continuum of care.

- Acceptance of documentation as an integral part of the treatment process.

- Willingness to use appropriate technology.

- Apply placement, continued stay, and discharge criteria for each modality on the continuum of care.

- Confidence in client's ability to progress within a continuum of care.

- Appreciation for the fair and objective use of client placement, continued stay, and discharge criteria.

Client, Family, and Community Education

Client, family, and community education is the process of providing clients, families, significant others, and community groups with information on risks related to substance use, as well as available prevention, treatment and recovery resources. Educating the client, family, and community provides culturally relevant formal and informal education programs that raise awareness and support substance abuse prevention and/or the recovery process.

Knowledge

- Cultural differences among ethnically and racially diverse communities.

- Cultural differences in consumption of psychoactive substances.

- Delivery of educational programs.

- Research and theory on prevention of substance abuse problems.

- Learning styles and teaching methods.

- Public speaking.

- Individual, community, and group risk and resiliency factors.

- Social issues influencing the development of substance abuse.

- Environmental influences on risk and resiliency

- Cultural issues in planning prevention and treatment programs.

- Age and gender differences in psychoactive substance use.
- Culture, gender, and age-appropriate prevention, treatment, and recovery resources.
- The continuum of use and abuse, including the warning signs and symptoms of a developing substance use disorder.
- Role of public policy in prevention and treatment of substance use disorders.
- Current DSM categories or other diagnostic standards associated with psychoactive substance use.
- How psychoactive substance use by one family member affects other family members or significant others.
- The family's potential positive or negative influence on the development and continuation of a substance use disorder.
- The role of the family, couple, or significant other in treatment and recovery.
- The continuum of care.
- Available treatment resources, including local health, allied health, and behavioral health resources.
- Models for prevention, treatment, and recovery from substance use disorders.
- Research and theory on models of prevention, treatment, and recovery.
- Influences on societal and political responses to substance use disorders.
- Health risks associated with substance use.
- High-risk behaviors related to substance use.
- Prevention and transmission of infectious diseases.
- Factors that may be associated with the prevention or transmission of infectious diseases.
- Community health and allied health resources.
- The importance of life skills to the prevention and treatment of substance use disorders.
- How these skills are typically taught to individuals and groups.
- Local resources available to teach these skills.

Skills

- Delivering prevention and treatment educational programs.
- Facilitating discussion.
- Preparing outlines and handout materials.
- Making public presentations.
- Describing individual, community, and group risk and resiliency factors.
- Communicating effectively with diverse populations.
- Providing educational programs that reflect understanding of culture, ethnicity, age, and gender.
- Teaching signs and symptoms of various substance use disorders.
- Facilitating discussions that outline the warning signs and symptoms of various substance use disorders.
- Educating clients, families, and the community about the impact of substance use disorders on the family, couple, or significant others.
- Motivating both family members and clients to seek care.
- Describing different treatment modalities and the continuum of care.
- Identifying and making referrals to local health, allied health, and behavioral health resources.
- Organizing and delivering presentations that reflect basic information on prevention, treatment, and recovery.
- Teaching clients and community members about disease transmission and prevention.
- Facilitating small and large group discussions.
- Implementing training sessions.
- Identifying and accessing other instructional resources for training.

Attitudes

- Awareness of and sensitivity to cultural differences.
- Appreciation of the difference between educating and providing information.
- Appreciating the historical, social, cultural, and other influences that shape

the perceptions of psychoactive substance use.

- Describe factors that increase the likelihood for an individual, community, or group to be at-risk for, or resilient to, psychoactive substance use disorders.

- Sensitivity to individual, community, and group differences in the risk for development of substance use disorders.

- Non-judgmental presentation of issues.

- Sensitize others to issues of cultural identity, ethnic background, age, and gender in prevention, treatment, and recovery.

- Sensitivity to the role of culture, ethnicity, age, and gender in prevention, treatment, and recovery.

- Awareness of one's own cultural biases.

- Describe warning signs, symptoms, and the course of substance use disorders.

- Recognition of the importance of research in prevention and treatment.

- Describe how substance use disorders affect families and concerned others.

- Recognition of the unique response of family members and significant others to substance use disorders.

- Describe the continuum of care and resources available to family and concerned others.

- Patience and perseverance.

- Appreciation of the difficulty for families and significant others to seek help.

- Appreciation of ethnic and cultural differences.

- Describe principles and philosophy of prevention, treatment, and recovery.

- Appreciation of the importance of prevention and treatment.

- Recognition of the validity of a variety of prevention and treatment strategies.

- Understand and describe the health and behavior problems related to substance use, including transmission and prevention of HIV/AIDS, TB, STDs, and other infectious diseases.

- Awareness of one's own biases when presenting this information.

- Teach life skills, including but not limited to, stress management, relaxation, communication, assertiveness, and refusal skills.

- Recognition of the importance of life skills training to the process of recovery.

Assessment & Psycho-Social-Spiritual Evaluation

- The counselor must develop the skills necessary to exhibit sensitivity to the patient during the initial assessment as well as during treatment in the aftercare process.

- The counselor must work closely with other professionals for optimal care of the recovering addict. This works by joining different techniques, in order to provide the best results.

- The counselor must provide treatment based on the unique needs of the patient, as this is the most vital part of the treatment process.

- All effective treatment programs must incorporate all therapies for the patient in order for the best results to occur.

- Appropriate changes must be made by different professionals working within the treatment program, and problems regarding mental health should be addressed.

- Through the treatment process, the counselor can properly address the different issues, and progressions can be noted.

Prevention and Stress Management

The prevention and stress management process involves regularly addressing feelings related to different areas of treatment, types of treatment, and negative emotions. Support groups are used to determine the appropriate way of preventing stress by working with others on a professional basis. These often involve long-term skill development. The patient must develop skills to reduce stress.

Clear Purpose and Goals

- Clearly define the counseling intervention goals and strategies appropriate for the client.
- Define community needs, focus, and scope of the program.

- Do a periodic assessment of the client's mental health and service targets and strategies.

- Integrate crisis counseling and guidance into service priorities.

- Train and supervise staff to define limits and make referrals, and have them provide feedback on number of contacts, program accomplishments, and other data.

- Staff should be oriented and trained with written role descriptions for each assignment setting.

Connecting Stress and Relapse

According to the National Institutes of Health, stress is a critical factor for using alcohol and drugs and a significant aspect of relapse. Treatment techniques to prevent relapse and manage stress include social support, developing coping skills, and adequate problem-solving abilities. SAMHSA reports that around 50 percent of persons recovering from drug or alcohol abuse will experience one relapse. Components that connect stress and relapse include:

- Lack of ability to handle social pressures

- Psychological and physical reminders of past use

- Frequent exposure to circumstances that lead to drug or alcohol use

- Insufficient skills for dealing with negative emotions or interpersonal conflict

Developing Coping Skills

One of the most important aspects of a client's recovery is the development of stress management techniques and adequate coping skills. Stress often arises from many situations that are detrimental to a person's health. For recovering addicts, stress is the impetus for relapse. A drug and alcohol treatment program will help the addict gain understanding in his or her individual triggers and learn how to handle those triggers in the future.

Stress Management Techniques

One way for a drug and alcohol counselor to assist a client with stress management is to help with the development of constructive hobbies and activities that do not involve substance use. Many clients struggle after they leave an addiction recover center because they are thrust back around social circles and circumstances associated with substance abuse. The client will have an improved chance of recovery by cultivating activities that do not involve this harmful behavior and to avoid such temptations.

For a successful recovery, the client should identify high-risk situations that could lead to stress and relapse before he or she leaves the rehabilitation center. Exercise is one good way to relieve stress, as it helps to cope with challenging circumstances. Nutrition is also an important aspect to help the client deal with negative emotions while also enhancing his or her overall well-being.

Group, family, and individual counseling or therapy has proven advantageous for persons who have trouble handing stress and who are prone to relapse due to poor coping abilities. Clients should be encouraged to discuss these problems with other people who are struggling with recovery from substance use.

Relapse Prevention Worksheet

Relapse does not start with the first drink or use of one drug. It has a progressive, destructive, behavioral pattern. The most commonly reported symptoms are listed on this relapse prevention worksheet. This can be used to assess the client for potential for relapse.

- *Return of Denial*
  1. Concern about well-being
  2. Denial of the concern

- *Avoidance and Defensive Behavior*
  1. Believing "I'll never drink again"
  2. Worrying about others instead of yourself
  3. Defensiveness
  4. Compulsive behavior
  5. Impulsive behavior
  6. Tendency toward loneliness

- *Crisis Building*

    1. Tunnel vision

    2. More depression

    3. Loss of constructive planning

    4. Plans begin to fail

- *Immobilization*

    1. Daydreaming and wishful thinking

    2. Feelings that nothing can be solved

    3. Immature wish to be happy

- *Confusion and Overreaction*

    1. Periods of confusion

    2. Irritation with friends

    3. Easily angered

- *Depression*

    1. Irregular eating habits

    2. Lack of desire to take action

    3. Irregular sleeping habits

    4. Loss of daily structure

    5. Periods of deep depression

    6. Irregular attendance at 12-Step meetings

    7. Development of an "I don't care" attitude.

    8. Open rejection of help

    9. Dissatisfaction with life

    10. Feelings of powerlessness and helplessness

- *Recognition of Loss of Control*

  1. Self-pity

  2. Thoughts of social drinking/drug using

  3. Conscious lying

  4. Complete loss of self-confidence

- *Option Reduction*

  1. Unreasonable resentments

  2. Discontinues all treatment

  3. Overwhelming loneliness, frustration, anger and tension

- *Acute Relapse Episode*

  1. Loss of Behavioral Control

  2. Acute relapse episode, marked by:

     a) Degeneration in all life areas

     b) Alcohol or drug use

     c) Emotional collapse

     d) Physical collapse

     e) Stress-related illness

     f) Psychiatric illness

     g) Suicide attempt

     h) Accident proneness

     i) Disruption of social structures

Professional Responsibility and Ethics
(45 Hours)

Overview

Ethics are complex when it comes to drug and alcohol addiction. Ethical practice for the alcoholism and substance abuse professional involves several steps that must be taken within the system to avoid problems or cause harm to the patient. The ethical principles are a set of principles that create moral decisions involving patient care and value to the patient during the care. Aspects of ethical practice include:

- *Moral decisions* - These are decisions made by a counselor in a manner that regards the patient's best interest. Decisions involve policy, the right attitude, and appropriate behaviors on a case-by-case basis.

- *Laws* - These are rules and regulations known as informal ethical decision-making policy regarding all substance abuse counselors.

- *Principles* - The principles involved with ethics are based on a vast understanding of the principles within the addictions field. According to the principle, just because something is legal doesn't mean it's ethical.

Counselors must understand the different issues that can occur within the counseling field and how various laws apply to the patient and the counselor. When working with patients in different states, counselors must consider each state and the specific area regulations regarding substance abuse and treatment in each state. This is done to determine the legal and ethical aspects around the situation.

Each state must provide a guideline, which contains specific information based on various state to state laws. Hard copies of ethical principles should be provided to all counselors and other professionals working within the field. The ethical guide contains informational education on the behavior that should take place within this position.

Several ethical issues are involved with behavioral stance, but there are three main areas of focuses. These include:

- Confidentiality issues

- Dual resistance

- Rebellion against legal and ethical issues.

Professionalism and Ethics

Professional and ethical responsibilities are the obligations of an addiction counselor to adhere to accepted ethical and behavioral standards of conduct and continuing professional development. Within this concept, the counselor must adhere to established professional codes of ethics that define the professional context within which the counselor works, in order to maintain professional standards and safeguard the client.

Knowledge

- Federal, State, agency, and professional codes of ethics.
- Client rights and responsibilities.
- Professional standards and scope of practice.
- Boundary issues between client and counselor.
- Difference between the role of the professional counselor and that of a peer counselor or sponsor.
- Consequences of violating codes of ethics.
- Means for addressing alleged ethical violations.
- Non-discriminatory practices.
- Mandatory reporting requirements.
- Federal, State, and agency regulations that apply to addiction counseling.
- Confidentiality regulations.
- Client rights and responsibilities.
- Legal ramifications of non-compliance with confidentiality regulations.
- Legal ramifications of violating client rights.
- Grievance processes.
- Professional literature on substance use disorders.
- Information on current trends in addiction and related fields.
- Professional associations.
- Resources to promote professional growth and competency.
- Differences found in diverse populations.

- How individual differences impact assessment and response to treatment.
- Personality, culture, lifestyle, and other factors influencing client behavior.
- Culturally sensitive counseling methods.
- Dynamics of family systems in diverse cultures and lifestyles.
- Client advocacy needs specific to diverse cultures and lifestyles.
- Signs, symptoms, and patterns of violence against persons.
- Risk factors that relate to potential harm to self or others.
- Hierarchy of needs and motivation.
- The role of supervision.
- Models of supervision.
- Potential barriers in the counselor and client relationship.
- Transference and countertransference.
- Resources for exploration of professional concerns.
- Problem-solving methods.
- Conflict resolution.
- The process and impact of client reassignment.
- The process and impact of termination of the counseling relationship.
- Phases of treatment and client responses.
- Personal and professional strengths and limitations.
- Legal, ethical, and professional standards affecting addiction counseling.
- Consequences of failure to comply with professional standards.
- Self-evaluation methods.
- Regulatory guidelines and restrictions.
- Education and training methods that promote professional growth.
- Recredentialing requirements.
- The rationale for regular assessment of professional skills and development.
- Models of clinical and administrative supervision.
- The rationale for using consultation.
- Agency policy and protocols.

- Case presentation methods.

- How to identify needs for clinical or technical assistance.

- Interpersonal dynamics in a supervisory relationship.

- Rationale for periodic self-assessment regarding physical and mental health.

- Available resources for maintaining physical and mental health.

- Consequences of failing to maintain physical and mental health.

- Relationship between physical and mental health.

- Health promotion strategies.

Skills

- Demonstrating ethical and professional behavior.

- Interpreting and applying appropriate Federal, State, and agency regulations regarding addiction counseling.

- Making ethical decisions that reflect unique needs and situations.

- Providing treatment services that conform to Federal, State, and local regulations.

- Reading and interpreting current professional and research-based literature.

- Applying professional knowledge to client-specific situations.

- Applying research findings to clinical practice.

- Applying new skills in clinically appropriate ways.

- Interest in expanding one's own knowledge and skills base.

- Willingness to adjust clinical practice to reflect advances in the field.

- Recognize the importance of individual differences that influence client behavior and apply this understanding to clinical practice.

- Assessing and interpreting culturally specific client behaviors and lifestyle.

- Conveying respect for cultural and lifestyle diversity in the therapeutic process.

- Adapting therapeutic strategies to client needs.

- Recognizing situations in which supervision is appropriate.

- Developing a plan for resolution or improvement.

- Seeking supervisory feedback.

- Resolving conflicts.

- Identifying overt and covert feelings and their impact on the counseling relationship.

- Communicating feelings and concerns openly and respectfully.

- Developing professional goals and objectives.

- Interpreting and applying ethical, legal, and professional standards.

- Using self-assessment tools for personal and professional growth.

- Eliciting and applying feedback from colleagues and supervisors.

- Assessing personal training needs.

- Selecting and participating in appropriate training programs.

- Using consultation and supervision as an enhancement to professional growth.

- Identifying professional progress and limitations.

- Communicating the need for assistance.

- Preparing and making case presentations.

- Eliciting feedback from others.

- Carrying out regular self-assessment with regards to physical and mental health.

- Using prevention measures to guard against burnout.

- Employing stress reduction strategies.

- Locating and accessing resources to achieve physical and mental health.

- Modeling self-care as an effective treatment tool.

Attitudes

- Openness to changing personal behaviors and attitudes that may conflict with ethical guidelines.

- Willingness to participate in self, peer, and supervisory assessment of clinical skills and practice.

- Respect for professional standards.

- Adhere to Federal and State laws and agency regulations regarding the treatment of substance use disorders.

- Appreciation of the importance of complying with Federal, State, and agency regulations.

- Willingness to learn appropriate application of Federal, State, and agency guidelines.

- Interpret and apply information from current counseling and psychoactive substance use research literature to improve client care and enhance professional growth.

- Interest in expanding one's own knowledge and skills base.

- Willingness to adjust clinical practice to reflect advances in the field.

- Recognize the importance of individual differences that influence client behavior and apply this understanding to clinical practice.

- Willingness to appreciate the life experiences of individuals.

- Appreciation for diverse populations and lifestyles.

- Recognition of one's own biases towards other cultures and lifestyles.

- Utilize a range of supervisory options to process personal feelings and concerns about clients.

- Willingness to accept feedback.

- Acceptance of responsibility for personal and professional growth.

- Awareness that one's own personal recovery issues have an impact on job performance and interactions with clients.

- Conduct self-evaluations of professional performance applying ethical, legal, and professional standards to enhance self-awareness and performance.

- Appreciation of the importance of self-evaluation.

- Recognition of personal strengths, weaknesses, and limitations.

- Willingness to change behaviors as necessary.

- Obtain appropriate continuing professional education.

- Recognition that professional growth continues throughout one's professional career.

- Willingness to expose oneself to information that may conflict with personal and/or professional beliefs.

- Recognition that professional development is an individual responsibility.
- Participate in ongoing supervision and consultation.
- Willingness to accept both constructive criticism and positive feedback.
- Respect for the value of clinical and administrative supervision.
- Develop and utilize strategies to maintain one's own physical and mental health.
- Recognition that counselors serve as role models.
- Appreciation that maintaining a healthy lifestyle enhances the counselor's effectiveness.

In order to maintain confidentiality when providing counseling to a patient with a substance abuse issue, any information received by the counselor is considered confidential and private. The information cannot be shared with other medical professionals even if they need the information for the further treatment of the patient. In order for the information to be provided to the medical professional, there must be a prior authorization provided by the patient.

Authorization is made when the patient signs a disclosure of records, which is done in the presence of the counselor who is providing the treatment to the patient. With the area of confidentiality regarding ethics, a judgment of privilege for proper administration of justice allows disclosure under certain exceptions. Certain examples of "duty to report" include suspected child abuse, or when the abuse of an adult is suspected to be severe or life-threatening.

Duty to Warn

Duty to warn is a process where the counselor providing treatment to the patient takes steps in order to determine whether serious danger is present. For example, if the patient is being abused physically, the potential of serious abuse must be identified and then reported to the appropriate agency. To assess the situation, the counselor should first talk to the supervisor in charge of the treatment plan to obtain assistance to make the correct decision. After this, the case should be referred to the police, so the potential victim can receive the care they need.

Proper Consent

In order to provide proper consent, the patient must be informed when an outside party needs to disclose information that was provided during counseling sessions. The patient does have the right to refuse the disclosure, but they must provide a written statement as to why they do not want to disclose that information to the other party. In certain cases, the law may be able to override the lack of providing disclosure, and the counselor must provide all information regarding the treatment of the patient. This is generally used when legal issues involve abuse problems or issues within the criminal justice system. In some cases where there is no harm, the judge could subpoena the counselor to provide the information.

In certain situations, verbal communication is not considered to be disclosure of information of the patient. This occurs when information is given to specific agencies such as other mental health facilities providing treatment to the patient.

If confidential counseling information is requested regarding an adolescent, the disclosure of the information is treated in the same way as with an adult. The minor must be informed regarding the request for the information, determine if they want to release information, and then both the parent and the minor must sign a consent form.

There are certain laws and ethical procedures involved with clinical charting. This can include the counselor's use of documentation in order to make progress notes for the client and on the counseling sessions. In order to correctly follow the legal and ethical concerns regarding documentation of the patient's information, the counselor must provide facts without releasing too much information regarding the treatment process.

Notation Guidelines

- Use black ink because it enables you to make copies that are easy to read.

- Take time to create notes that are easy-to-read. A logical, well written document will have a clear pattern, appropriate paragraphs, and good grammar. Some notes may be typed in order to provide the most clearly written information. By taking this step, you could reduce misunderstanding of the notes and avoid adverse effects.

- Different agencies use different note formats. These are formed during note writing, and the note writing format used by the agency should be used at all times by the counselor.

- While choosing words, it is important that the worst issues are documented carefully, and the emphasis is placed on important areas, such as when the patient had made statements or reports.

- Use enough information with envelopes so that the concept of the session can be captured. However, avoid excessive note-taking.

- While creating the notes, take into consideration the future readers, such as healthcare providers, court reporters, or legal professionals.

Documentation

Proper documentation involves recording the screening and intake process, assessment, treatment plan, clinical reports, clinical progress notes, discharge summaries, and other client-related data.

These include, but are not limited to: psychoactive substance use and abuse history, physical health, psychological information, social information, history of criminality, spiritual information, recreational information, nutritional information, educational and/or vocational information, sexual information, and legal information.

The Discharge Summary

The components of a discharge summary include but not limited to: client profile and demographics, presenting symptoms, diagnoses, selected interventions, critical incidents, progress toward treatment goals, outcome, aftercare plan, prognosis, and recommendations.

Knowledge

- Regulations pertaining to client records.

- The essential components of client records, including release forms, assessments, treatment plans, progress notes, and discharge summaries and plans.

- Program, State, and Federal confidentiality regulations.

- The application of confidentiality regulations.

- Confidentiality regulations regarding infectious diseases.

- The legal nature of records

- Current Federal, State, local, and program regulations.

- Regulations regarding informed consent.

- Appropriate clinical terminology used to describe client progress.

- How to review and update records.

- Accepted measures of treatment outcome.

- Current research related to defining treatment outcomes.

- Methods of gathering outcome data.

- Principles of using outcome data for program evaluation.

- Distinctions between process and outcome evaluation.

Skills

- Composing timely, clear, and concise records that comply with regulations.

- Documenting information in an objective manner.
- Writing legibly.
- Utilizing new technologies in the production of client records.
- Applying Federal, State, and agency regulations regarding client confidentiality.
- Requesting, preparing, and completing release of information when appropriate.
- Protecting and communicating client rights.
- Explaining regulations to clients and third parties.
- Applying infectious disease regulations as they relate to addictions treatment.
- Providing security for clinical records.
- Analyzing, synthesizing, and summarizing information.
- Recording information that is concise and relevant.
- Documenting timely, clear, and concise records that comply with regulations
- Preparing clear and legible documents.
- Documenting changes in the treatment plan.
- Using appropriate clinical terminology.
- Summarizing information.
- Preparing concise discharge summaries.
- Completing timely records.
- Reporting measurable results.
- Gathering and recording outcome data.
- Incorporating outcome measures during the treatment process.

Attitudes
- Appreciation of the importance of accurate documentation.
- Protect client rights to privacy and confidentiality in the preparation and handling of records, especially in relation to the communication of client information with third parties.

- Willingness to seek and accept supervision regarding confidentiality regulations.

- Respect for the client's right to privacy and confidentiality.

- Commitment to professionalism.

- Recognition of the absolute necessity of safeguarding records.

- Prepare accurate and concise screening, intake, and assessment reports.

- Willingness to develop accurate reports.

- Recognition of the importance of accurate records.

- Record treatment and continuing care plans that are consistent with agency standards and comply with applicable administrative rules.

- Recognition of the importance of recording treatment and continuing care plans.

- Record progress of client in relation to treatment goals and objectives.

- Recognition of the value of objectively recording progress.

- Recognition that timely recording is critical to accurate documentation.

- Prepare accurate and concise discharge summaries.

- Recognition that treatment is not a static, singular event.

- Recognition that recovery is ongoing.

- Recognition that timely recording is critical to accurate documentation.

- Document treatment outcome, using accepted methods and instruments.

- Recognition that treatment and evaluation should occur simultaneously.

- Appreciation of the importance of using data to improve clinical practice.

Ethics & Counselor Responsibilities

Practicum students are expected to act in an ethical manner consistent with the Ethical Standards of the American Counseling Association. In practicum, you will experience the application of these various standards and procedures. This process involves:

- Personal information

- Informed consent

- Authorization for audio/video recording

- Protection of client anonymity

To protect the client's anonymity, their names are not to be used, and students should avoid documenting information that would disclose identity. Written permission should be obtained in the form of a signature before recording starts. When counseling minors, the guardian or parent should consent for participation. The practicum student should be cautious to obtain appropriate consultation when instances occur outside of his or her range of competency.

CACREP Vision and Mission

The overall goal of practicum is for the student counselor to gain experience, integrate past learning experiences, develop competencies, increase self-awareness and gain insight into theory and technique. As an accrediting body, the Counseling for the Accreditation of Counseling and Related Educational Programs (CACREP) develops standards and procedures that reflect the needs of a complex and diverse society. They are dedicated to:

- Encouraging and promoting the continuing development and improvement of preparation programs.

- Preparing counselors and related professionals to provide services consistent with the ideal of optimal human development, and promoting their professional competence through the development of preparation standards, the encouragement of excellence in program development and the accreditation of professional preparation programs.

CACREP Clinical Mental Health Counseling Practicum Standards

- Demonstrates the ability to apply and adhere to ethical and legal standards in clinical mental health counseling.

- Uses the principles and practices of diagnosis, treatment, referral, and prevention of mental and emotional disorders to initiate, maintain, and terminate counseling.

- Applies multicultural competencies to clinical mental health counseling involving case conceptualization, diagnosis, treatment, referral, and prevention of mental and emotional disorders.

- Applies effective strategies to promote client understanding of and access to a variety of community resources.

- Demonstrates appropriate use of culturally responsive individual, couple, family, group, and systems modalities for initiating, maintaining, and terminating counseling.

- Demonstrates the ability to use procedures for assessing and managing suicide risk.

- Applies current record-keeping standards related to clinical mental health counseling.

- Provides appropriate counseling strategies when working with clients with addiction and co- occurring disorders.

- Demonstrates the ability to recognize his or her own limitations as a clinical mental health counselor and to seek supervision or refer clients when appropriate.

- Maintains information regarding community resources to make appropriate referrals.

- Demonstrates the ability to modify counseling systems, theories, techniques, and interventions to make them culturally appropriate for diverse populations.

- Demonstrates skill in conducting an intake interview, a mental status evaluation, a biopsychosocial history, a mental health history, and a psychological assessment for treatment planning and caseload management.

- Screens for addiction, aggression, and danger to self and/or others, as well as co-occurring mental disorders.

- Analyzes assessment information in a manner that produces valid inferences when evaluating the needs of individual students and assessing the effectiveness of educational programs.

- Makes appropriate referrals to school and/or community resources.

- Assesses barriers that impede students' academic, career, and personal/social development.

- Works with parents, guardians, and families to act on behalf of their children to address problems that affect student success in school.

- Locates resources in the community that can be used in the school to improve student achievement and success.

- Consults with teachers, staff, and community-based organizations to promote student academic, career, and personal/social development.

- Uses referral procedures to secure assistance for students and their families.

Practice Examination

1. To understand addiction, the counselor must comprehend which aspects of addiction?

A. Social

B. Economic

C. Cultural

D. All of the above

Answer: D. All of the above

Explanation: The counselor must understand the social, economic, and cultural aspects of addiction.

2. According to researchers, the concept of addiction something caused by:

A. The mood of the patient.

B. The psychological state of the patient.

C. The physical state of the patient.

D. All of the above

Answer: B. The psychological state of the patient.

Explanation: According to researchers, the concept of addiction is known to be something caused by the psychological state of the patient. Addiction to drugs presents itself psychologically, in a manner that is similar to other forms of addiction, such as gambling.

3. What should be used to evaluate and assess the patient's addiction?

A. Biomarkers

B. Laboratory testing

C. Patient's own report of substance use

D. Counselor's opinion of substance use

Answer: A. Biomarkers

Explanation: Biomarkers are the best indicators of substance use. Biomarkers will allow you to track a patient's recovery process and identify risks of addiction based upon previous psychological patterns and behaviors. Biomarkers can be detected in both urine and blood tests. These can be used to detect if the patient is using on occasion or if heavy use is present.

4. The elements involved in the psychological aspect of addiction include all of the following EXCEPT:

A. Sense of powerlessness

B. Sense of hopelessness

C. Sense of rage

D. Sense of accomplishment

Answer: D. Sense of accomplishment

Explanation: There are three different elements contained within the psychological aspect of addiction. With a sense of powerlessness, addiction is often accompanied by feelings of helplessness and powerlessness. The feeling is often experienced after the use of the substance. With a sense of rage, there is an angry feeling that people experience when they suffer emotional injury, and acts as fuel for substance abuse. The rage may cause the person to show irrational, destructive behavioral patterns.

5. What is the term for using a drug in a manner or for a reason that differs from how it was prescribed, which is often unintentional?

A. Misuse

B. Abuse

C. Dependence

D. Tolerance

Answer: A. Misuse

Explanation: Misuse is using a drug in a manner, or for a reason. that differs from how it was prescribed. Misuse is unintentional.

6. Physical dependence occurs when:

A. Drug or alcohol abuse has occurred for a prolonged period, and the person can become both mentally and physically addicted to the drug.

B. A person has a strong mental urge to use a drug to experience the effects considered to be pleasant (drug or alcohol used to reach a euphoric state of mind).

C. A person may use another drug form to lessen the withdrawal they are experiencing from their drug of choice.

D. A person's body is used to taking the drug, and they start to experience withdrawal symptoms when the drug is no longer present in their system.

Answer: D. A person's body is used to taking the drug, and they start to experience withdrawal symptoms when the drug is no longer present in their system.

Explanation: Dependence is a state that occurs when abuse has occurred for a prolonged time. The person can become both mentally and physically addicted. Psychological dependence is a strong mental urge to use a drug to experience effects considered to be pleasant (drugs or alcohol used to reach a euphoric state of mind). Cross-dependence is where a person may use another drug form to lessen the withdrawal they are experiencing from their drug of choice. Physical dependence occurs when a person's body is used to taking the drug, and they start to experience withdraw symptoms when the drug is no longer present in their system.

7. The amount of time the drug stays present within the body is called the:

A. Dose

B. Half-life

C. Lethal dose

D. Therapeutic dose

Answer: B. Half-life

Explanation: The half-life is the amount of time the drug stays present within the body. This level can be affected based upon metabolism and other factors, which differ from the specific half-life of the drug.

8. Drug interactions can occur between:

A. Street drugs

B. Prescription drugs

C. Alcohol

D. All of the above

Answer: All of the above

Explanation: A drug interaction is the way that drugs interact with one another. This includes interactions between street drugs, prescription drugs, and alcohol.

9. Using a drug in a manner other than that prescribed, with the intention of getting high, is called:

A. Use

B. Misuse

C. Abuse

D. Dependence

Answer: C. Abuse

Explanation: Abuse is using a drug in a manner other than that prescribed, with the intention of getting high, such as taking too much of one drug within a short period of time.

10. This can cause a person to become more sensitive to the drug over a period of time:

A. Physical dependence

B. Tolerance

C. Abuse

D. Reverse tolerance

Answer: D. Reverse tolerance

Explanation: Reverse tolerance can cause a person to become more sensitive to the drug over a period of time, rather than less sensitive. It will cause the substance to have a higher level of impact on the person when taken.

11. Regarding drug administration, what is considered to be the most rapid method of action for a substance?

A. Oral

B. Intravenous

C. Injection

D. Snorting (intranasal)

Answer: B. Intravenous

Explanation: The way the drug is administered can affect its method of action. A drug will be stronger when taken intravenously, compared to the oral, injection, or intranasal administration methods.

12. What is a danger of intranasal (snorting) drug administration?

A. Severe damage to the sinus cavity

B. Brain damage

C. Both A and B

D. Neither A nor B

Answer: C. Both A and B

Explanation: Snorting is commonly used among those who abuse oral medications. While the effects are fast acting, the side-effects can be very dangerous, and in some cases, deadly. Those who use this method of administration can cause severe damage to occur within the sinus cavity, and brain damage can also occur with both short and prolonged usage.

13. What can occur if a time-release medication is crushed or the capsule is opened so the components can be taken?

A. Too little of the medication will be provided during one period of time.

B. Too much of the medication will be provided during one period of time.

C. Both A and B

D. Neither A nor B

Answer: B. Too much of the medication will be provided during one period of time.

Explanation: Some medications that are taken orally have restrictions that make it necessary for the medication to be taken orally. A time-released medication will need to be taken by mouth and cannot be crushed, or the time release action will be disrupted.

14. Why would someone desire to use cocaine in a suppository or rectal form?

A. The mucus membranes in the rectum area can absorb some drugs quickly.

B. The nerve endings in the rectum area can absorb some drugs quickly.

C. The mucus membranes in the rectum area make the drug more potent.

D. The nerve endings in the rectum make the drug more potent.

Answer: A. The mucus membranes in the rectum area can absorb some drugs quickly.

Explanation: While not all drugs can be taken rectally, certain drugs such as cocaine can be taken through a suppository. The mucus membranes in the rectum area can absorb some drugs quickly. This method is used by those looking to receive the drug quickly, but this can be risky.

15. These types of injections are done by injecting the drug of choice into the soft tissue present under the skin:

A. Intramuscular

B. Intravenous

C. Intradermal

D. Subcutaneous

Answer: D. Subcutaneous

Explanation: Subcutaneous injections are done by injecting the drug of choice into the soft tissue present under the skin.

16. What types of drug requires eating or drinking for administration?

A. Certain types of mushrooms

B. LSD

C. Alcohol

D. All of the above

Answer: D. All of the above

Explanation: Drinking is common with alcohol, but certain drugs need to be eaten in order for them to work properly. For example, the illegal street drug LSD requires you to eat the drug in order for it to work, as do "magic mushrooms."

17. Infections can occur during injection drug administration due to:

A. Use of cotton that gets stuck within the syringe.

B. Lack of proper preparation.

C. An unsterile injection site.

D. All of the above

Answer: D. All of the above

Explanation: The risk of an infection is also high when using the injection method, as many drugs require the use of cotton while they are prepared, and this can lead to the cotton getting stuck within the syringe, and being placed under the skin. Infections can also occur due to lack of proper preparation, which creates an unsterile environment when the needle is injected into the skin.

18. Regarding toxicology testing, when should urine testing be done?

A. Within two days of the drug use

B. Within three days of the drug use

C. Within four days of the drug use

D. Within five days of the drug use

Answer: D. Within five days of the drug use

Explanation: Urine testing must be done within five days of drug use, as the drug begins to leave the urine at this time and an accurate test cannot be conducted.

19. Which type of toxicology testing is the most effective for drugs?

A. Blood testing

B. Saliva testing

C. Hair testing

D. Urine testing

Answer: A. Blood testing

Explanation: To perform blood testing, a blood sample is taken from the patient with a syringe. This method of testing is one of the most effective for drugs, as drugs can be detected in the blood much faster than urine and saliva, and they also stay in the blood for longer periods of time.

20. This type of toxicology testing is done by using the swab on the inside of the cheek, and then enclosing the swab in a sterilized container that will be sent to a lab for testing:

A. Swab testing

B. Saliva testing

C. Cheek testing

D. Container testing

Answer: B. Saliva testing

Explanation: With saliva testing, a swab made from cotton material is used to take a sample of the saliva that is found in the mouth. The mucus membranes within the mouth will have traces of the drug, which will then move into the saliva. This testing is done by using the swab on the inside of the cheek, and then enclosing the swab in a sterilized container that will be sent to a lab for testing.

21. How many drugs can be assessed with blood toxicology testing?

A. Up to three

B. Up to five

C. Up to fifteen

D. Up to thirty

Answer: D. Up to thirty

Explanation: Drug testing in any of these forms can be done to check for one specific drug, or to check for up to 30 drugs at one time.

22. The toxicology testing method depends upon:

A. The patient's report of use

B. The reason for testing

C. The counselor's preference

D. All of the above

Answer: B. The reason for testing

Explanation: The drug testing method used depends upon why it is being done. For example, if the test is taken for legal purposes, the examiner will look for a variety of drugs. However, when being used to help with addiction, one specific drug or those in a similar class are the focus.

23. Signs of addiction with impairment include all of the following EXCEPT:

A. Inability to keep a job or attend school

B. Use of substances in high risk situations, such as while driving

C. Legal consequences due to use of drugs

D. Having depression due to alcohol or substance use

Answer: D. Having depression due to alcohol or substance use.

Explanation: Two people using the same substance can have completely different reactions. Addiction is present when the individual has impairment due to the use of the substance. Impairment causes inability to keep a job or attend school, use of substances in high risk situations, such as while driving, legal consequences due to use of drugs, and encountering conflicts due to alcohol of substance use.

24. Which of the following does NOT play a role in biological addiction?

A. Tolerance

B. Genetics

C. Biochemistry

D. Metabolism

Answer: A. Tolerance

Explanation: The biological concept of addiction is based upon genetic factors that influence addiction. Genetics, biochemistry, and metabolism all play a role in addiction factors. Similar to the reaction that some people have to certain foods, some people may be unable to tolerate alcohol, even in small amounts.

25. What enzyme is thought to play a role in the susceptibility to alcohol abuse due to genetic disposition?

A. BYOB

B. MYOB

C. CYOB

D. DYOB

Answer: B. MYOB

Explanation: When addiction occurs based on genetic factors, signs of addiction often show before the substance is used. The enzyme MYOB may be lower in the brain of those who are susceptible to alcohol abuse due to their genetic disposition.

26. According to research studies, people with severe mental illnesses only experience success with recovery:

A. 10 percent of the time

B. 20 percent of the time

C. 35 percent of the time

D. 50 percent of the time

Answer: D. 50 percent of the time

Explanation: According to research studies, people with severe mental illnesses only experience success with recovery one-half of the time.

27. The addiction advocacy movement was created in order to provide recovery to patients by:

A. Involving the interdisciplinary team

B. Involving the patient's significant other

C. Involving the counselor

D. Involving the patient's family

Answer: D. Involving the patient's family

Explanation: The addiction advocacy movement was created in order to provide recovery to patients by involving their families in order to create a more personalized approach. When connection with families is used as part of a treatment program, long-term recovery is achievable, as this type of plan allows the patients to receive support from their family members while undergoing the recovery process.

28. The concept of recovery in addiction is:

A. A plan that works by implementing a treatment program that provides transformational change in those who are going through the process of recovery.

B. A plan that works by assessing the patient for transformational change while going through the process of recovery.

C. A plan that works by implementing an outpatient program that provides knowledge of addiction.

D. None of the above

Answer: A. A plan that works by implementing a treatment program that provides transformational change in those who are going through the process of recovery.

Explanation: As patient knowledge continues to expand, the methods used to treat addiction also expand and various techniques used together can provide recovery to patients in a treatment program.

29. Regarding substance abuse education and treatment, who could benefit from primary prevention measures?

A. Adolescents

B. Young people

C. Individuals with little or no history of drug and/or alcohol abuse.

D. All of the above

Answer: All of the above

Explanation: Primary prevention is used for young people or those with little to no history of drug/alcohol abuse.

30. Which of the following is NOT one of the primary prevention measures?

A. Promoting abstinence from drugs and alcohol.

B. Teaching refusal skills to those who haven't used.

C. Decreasing the age of usage, such as age limit to buy alcohol.

D. Providing education on the dangers associated with drugs and alcohol use.

Answer: C. Decreasing the age of usage, such as age limit to buy alcohol.

Explanation: Choices A, B, and D are all primary prevention measures, as are increasing the age of usage and promoting safe alternatives by offering community activities to the younger generation.

31. Reducing the available supply of drugs and alcohol through appropriate measures, including legal assistance, is a form of:

A. Recovery

B. Prevention

C. Treatment

D. Assessment

Answer: B. Prevention

Explanation: Preventive methods include reducing the available supply of drugs and alcohol through appropriate measures, including legal assistance, reducing the amount of demand present for drugs and alcohol by providing those in the community with appropriate treatment methods, and continuing development of treatment centers to improve the level of care offered.

32. Providing education on the risks, dangers, and other negative factors associated with use and abuse is an example of:

A. Primary prevention

B. Secondary prevention

C. Tertiary prevention

D. All of the above

Answer: B. Secondary prevention

Explanation: Secondary prevention is used to help addicts stop once early usage is detected by way of the HALT Theory. These measures include use intervention method to stop drug/substance use and abuse, education on the risks, dangers, and other negative factors associated with use and abuse, and skill-building techniques to help the client refrain from further use and abuse.

33. The counselor uses a specialized approach to treatment that includes desensitizing users to triggers, such as people, places, things, and actions. What type of prevention is this?

A. Primary prevention

B. Secondary prevention

C. Tertiary prevention

D. Quaternary prevention

Answer: C. Tertiary prevention

Explanation: Using a specialized approach to treatment which includes desensitizing users to triggers, such as people, places, things, and actions is a form of tertiary prevention. Tertiary prevention is used when drug or alcohol use and abuse has become progressive, and promotes healing of the mind and body.

34. The counselor teaches the 12 step principles to the patient in order to prepare him or her for leaving treatment after completion. What form of prevention is this?

A. Primary prevention

B. Secondary prevention

C. Tertiary prevention

D. Quaternary prevention

Answer: C. Tertiary prevention

Explanation: Creating a solid aftercare program for additional treatment once the initial program is complete is a form of tertiary prevention, as is teaching the 12 step principles to the patient in order to prepare him or her once treatment is complete.

35. This process involves meeting with the family and significant others of the addict:

A. Intervention

B. Cooperation

C. Location

D. Direction

Answer: A. Intervention

Explanation: Intervention is a process in which a group of people work together in order to interrupt addiction. This offers addicts several options to stop the process of addiction. Intervention can prevent the individual from hitting rock bottom, and it works to reorient those who have lost touch with reality.

36. This person uses substances heavily, but hasn't seen negative effects occur in health or life:

A. Moderate and non-problematic user

B. Heavy and non-problematic user

C. Heavy user with moderate problems

D. Heavy user with serious problems

Answer: B. Heavy and non-problematic user

Explanation: A non-user is a person who has not used substances. A moderate or non-problematic user is a person who uses some substances occasionally, but the use has not had a negative effect so far. A heavy and non-problematic user is a person who uses substances heavily, but hasn't seen negative effects. Heavy with serious problems is a person who uses substances very often, and has had many negative events occur. Heavy with moderate problems is a person who uses often and has had a few issues occur. Dependent and addicted with life and health problems is a person who is unable to stop drugs due to physical and mental addiction, and the use and abuse of substances has caused issues in the patients personal life, as well as had a negative effect on their health.

37. The correct order for the steps for treating addiction is:

A. Assess, identify, stabilize, rehabilitate

B. Identify, stabilize, rehabilitate, assess

C. Identify, assess, stabilize, rehabilitate

D. Stabilize, assess, rehabilitate, identify

Answer: C. Identify, assess, stabilize, rehabilitate

Explanation: Providing treatment for addiction requires the following steps in order for it to be effective: Step 1 - Identify: Screen the areas of the patient's life being effected from the addiction and identify the level of addiction present in the patient. Step 2 - Assess: Collect various pieces of information from the patient, and those involved in the patient's treatment plan identify patient's strengths, weaknesses, and treatment goals. Step 3 - Stabilize: Stop addiction to the substances using appropriate methods. Step 4 - Rehabilitate: Determine the proper long-term treatment program for the patient based upon their individual issues.

38. This rehabilitation program is typically used for patients that have successfully completed an inpatient or outpatient rehab program:

A. Co-occurring treatment program

B. Aftercare program

C. Intense care program

D. Self-help program

Answer: B. Aftercare program

Explanation: Co-occurring treatment centers offer treatment to patients who have mental health and substance abuse issues. Inpatient facilities are designed to treat patients who stay at the facility over the course of treatment. Outpatient facilities allow the patient to leave the facility and go home after the treatment is completed each day. Aftercare program are used for patients that have successfully completed an inpatient or outpatient rehab program.

39. This rehabilitation program is a fellowship for families who are not addicts, but who have one in their family, and members are trying to understand the addiction and how they can manage their own lives:

A. Al-Anon

B. Alcoholics Anonymous

C. Al-Teen

D. Al-Alc

Answer: A. Al-Anon

Explanation: Alcoholics Anonymous (AA) is a fellowship of men and women who come together in order to share their experiences, strength and hope for recovery. The only requirement to join this is to have the desire to stop drinking. Narcotics Anonymous (NA) is a non-profit organization meant for men and women who face major drug problems. The meetings are held in order to help maintain sobriety. Al-Teen is a fellowship for younger family members that work off of the same principles as Al-Anon.

40. HIV:

A. Has the fastest transition rate among all STDs.

B. Is most common among those who use drugs in the form of administering them with syringe for injection.

C. Is a growing epidemic among IV drug users.

D. All of the above

Answer: D. All of the above

Explanation: HIV is a virus that is contagious and can be spread from one person to another via blood and body fluids. This is a growing epidemic among IV drug users. Studies show that the HIV has the fastest transition rate among all other sexually transmitted diseases (STDs). It is most common among those who use drugs in the form of administering them with syringe for injection. Early cases of HIV often occur when sexual contact involves the use of drugs.

41. Which of the following is NOT one of the modes of HIV transmission?

A. Sexual intercourse

B. Saliva exchange

C. Sharing needles

D. Sharing hairbrushes

Answer: D. Sharing hairbrushes

Explanation: During intercourse, the HIV virus is transmitted between people through the mucous membranes in the rectum and vagina. Transmission can occur through the transfer of saliva. While this is less likely, it is still a possibility. When blood is caught within the needle and injected directly into the non-infected user's vein, this will almost always cause an HIV infection.

42. Of the following, which is NOT a sign that a recovering addict is ready for vocational rehabilitation?

A. She shows ongoing sobriety.

B. She understands why vocational rehabilitation is needed.

C. She recognizes that substance use is likely to recur.

D. She addresses entry issues as part of a better life goal plan.

Answer: C. She recognizes that substance use is likely to recur.

Explanation: A recovering addict will show readiness for vocational rehabilitation when he or she: recognizes abuse and involvement in the treatment program, shows commitment to recovery, shows progress towards achievement of goals and areas of employment, shows ongoing sobriety, addresses entry issues as part of a better life goal plan, understands why vocational rehabilitation is needed, addresses entry issues as part of a better life call, understands why vocational rehabilitation is an effective program for maintaining sobriety, and is able to independently complete process keeping a job.

43. The counselor assists the patient to learn he has much to offer in terms of helping others, as this will boost self-esteem. What therapeutic technique is this?

A. Bonding

B. Creating hope

C. Education

D. Altruism

Answer: D. Altruism

Explanation: Creating hope is where the counselor offers information and encouragement that things will get better. With bonding, the counselor offers connection that allows the patient to realize they are not alone. Education gives the patient an opportunity to learn about illness, symptoms, and behaviors from group members. Altruism is where the counselor assists the patient to learn they have much to offer in terms of helping others, as this will boost self-esteem.

44. The counselor wants to use a therapeutic technique for expression. What should he do?

A. Discuss events and feelings as the main focus of the group.

B. Encourage members of group to reconnect with important people in their life who were lost due to the addiction, such as close friends and family members.

C. Help members to listen and take part in different group activities in order to improve or reconnect with their social skills, such as taking part in role playing activities.

D. Group members will have deep fears and hidden feelings arise during the discussions, which will allow these issues to be addressed and worked through.

Answer: A. Discuss events and feelings as the main focus of the group.

Explanation: The counselor must work to encourage expression of group members' emotions in a positive manner.

45. The first step for immediate crisis intervention is:

A. Provide support to the recovering addict.

B. Initiate an intervention.

C. Offer hope with positive statements.

D. Provide a solution to the problem.

Answer: B. Initiate an intervention

Explanation: The immediate crisis intervention steps are: 1) initiate the intervention; 2) offer hope to the patient with positive statements; 3) provide support to the recovering addict; 4) provide a solution to problem immediately; and 5) give feedback to the patient in a positive manner.

46. The counselor puts himself in the patient's shoes in order to develop understanding of addiction and related problems. What is this technique?

A. Reflection

B. Active listening

C. Empathy

D. Paraphrasing

Answer: C. Empathy

Explanation: To offer empathy, the counselor must put himself in the patient's shoes in order to develop a true understanding of addiction and related problems.

47. In order to encourage the patient to explain things in further detail, the counselor should:

A. Use reflection

B. Use cues

C. Use open-ended questions

D. Use summarization

Answer: C. Use open-ended questions

Explanation: Leave questions open-ended in order to encourage the patient to explain things in further detail and develop a deeper understanding.

48. This type of therapy uses different methods to encourage the patient to take part in activities designed to change overall patterns of thinking, behavior, and methods of handling issues faced throughout the recovery process:

A. Cognitive therapy

B. Talk therapy

C. Hypnosis therapy

D. Psychoanalysis

Answer: A. Cognitive therapy

Explanation: Cognitive therapy addresses patterns of thinking and behavior, and methods of handling issues throughout the recovery process. Talk therapy creates a secure and effective environment where the patient can discuss his or her issues in confidence, and the therapist can offer encouragement, support, and positive coping techniques. Hypnosis/EMDR approaches are designed to change the patient's subconscious mind though special techniques, which allow that area of the mind to be accessed. Some professionals feel these two methods can offer lasting change, because they can help the patient deal with issues they were not aware existed.

49. The counselor determines reasons why a family is dysfunctional, examines problems and figures out a solution for better family dynamics. What type of counseling technique is used here?

A. Education

B. Joining

C. Structured analysis

D. All of the above

Answer: C. Structured analysis

Explanation: With education, resources are provided to the patient and family members. The recovering addict can utilize outside resources in order to continue on a successful recovery path. Joining involves the ability to connect, understand, and build strength within the families. This helps the recovering addict see how his or her recovery and behavior change can impact the family and how these things interact with one another.

50. Which is a true statement concerning domestic abuse battering?

A. Battering is secondary to a mental disorder.

B. Battering is only caused by substance use and abuse.

C. Battering is done because the perpetrator suffers from low self-esteem.

D. Battering is caused by loss of emotion.

Answer: C. Battering is done because the perpetrator suffers from low self-esteem.

Explanation: Abusers know it is wrong, and batter in order to feel better about themselves. Abuse is a learned behavior, and many times, the abuser will have suffered abuse in the past. This person uses force to gain control.

51. This treatment technique for domestic violence is used as a process to determine how each person within the relationship views abuse:

A. Funneling

B. Interviewing

C. Emotional expression

D. Assertiveness

Answer: A. Funneling

Explanation: This is done during individual or couple sessions in order to get information on all aspects involving the abuse, which is generally provided over time in small pieces.

52. During which stage of the cycle of abuse does the abuser often become apologetic?

A. Stage 1

B. Stage 2

C. Stage 3

D. Stage 4

Answer: C. Stage 3

Explanation: Stage 1: Increased tension is where there is an increase in the amount of tension that occurs within the household. Stage 2: Violence is when the domestic violence occurs. Stage 3: The compensation is where the abuser may become apologetic. Once forgiven, or forgotten, it will almost always start back at stage one. It's important to teach the victim this cycle and how to watch for increased tension again.

53. This term refers to the tendency for some people to use substances when they believe abstinence is too difficult to achieve or maintain:

A. Abstinence violation effect (AVE)

B. Substance reuse effect (SRE)

C. Abstinence reuse effect (ARE)

D. Substance violation effect (SVE)

Answer: A. Abstinence violation effect (AVE)

Explanation: AVE relates to what happens when a person attempting to abstain from a negative habitual behavior, such as drug use, engages in the behavior, and then faces conflict and guilt by making internal attributions to explain why he or she did it.

54. One very common trait among addicts of all backgrounds is:

A. A complete lack of money

B. A complete lack of family

C. A complete lack of spirituality

D. A complete lack of direction

Answer: C. A complete lack of spirituality

Explanation: The most common issue seen with addiction is a complete lack of spirituality in the patient. Many times, when addiction has become prolonged, negative, and life changing, the patient can experience a disconnection from themselves and from their prior spiritual beliefs.

55. When providing addiction treatment, the counselor should:

A. Avoid pushing the patient into spiritual beliefs during the treatment process.

B. Refer the patient to spiritual groups if he or she chooses to take that approach.

C. Allow the patient to guide conversations about spirituality.

D. All of the above

Answer: All of the above

Explanation: All of these things should be involved when providing addiction treatment. The counselor cannot push spirituality in order to encourage it within the patient. However, during the initial assessment of the patient, and in order to determine what the patient's feelings toward spirituality are, the counselor should assess this aspect of recovery.

56. Change can be observed in the addict by all of the following EXCEPT:

A. The patient will take part in interconnected change and self-discovery.

B. The patient will continue to have doubts throughout the entire recovery process.

C. The patient will develop an action plan that he or she will use during all times of the recovery.

D. The patient will maintain hope throughout the recovery process by using positive coping skills that he or she has developed.

Answer: B. The patient will continue to have doubts throughout the entire recovery process.

Explanation: Change is observed when the patient makes a connection between his or her life problems and the process of addiction, develops an action plan, takes part in interconnected change and self-discovery, develops a positive self-attitude and maintains it during and after the recovery, maintains hope by using positive coping skills and continues to keep perspective, even during difficult times.

57. During which stage of change does the patient plan to make a change, even if he or she has failed recently or in the past?

A. Stage 1 - Precontemplation

B. Stage 2 - Preparation

C. Stage 3 - Action

D. Stage 4 - Maintenance

Answer: B. Stage 2 - Preparation

Explanation: During stage 2 - Preparation, the patient plans to make a change, but may have failed recently or in the past. The patient may have created an incomplete plan and actively participated in it. In this stage, the patient makes small, insignificant changes.

58. During this stage, major changes are made, and relaxation is no longer an issue for the patient, as he or she continues to be active in recovery:

A. Stage 1 - Precontemplation

B. Stage 2 - Action

C. Stage 4 - Maintenance

D. Stage 5 - Termination

Answer: D. Stage 5 - Termination

Explanation: Stage 5 - Termination: During the fifth stage, major changes are made. Relaxation is no longer an issue for the patient, as he or she continues to be active in recovery. Although termination can be achieved with the right mind frame, complete termination is often seen as difficult to reach, because addiction is considered to be a life-long, ongoing process of change that needs to be maintained at all times.

59. How many phases of motivational counseling are there?

A. 3

B. 4

C. 5

D. 6

Answer: A. 3

Explanation: The phases are 1) empathy, 2) discrepancy, and 3) resistance.

60. The counselor works with the patient in order to help him develop love and trust in himself. By developing this, the patient is creating external and internal support. What type of motivational counseling is this?

A. Empathy

B. Discrepancy

C. Resistance

D. None of the above

Answer: B. Discrepancy

Explanation: During phase 2 - discrepancy, the phase is often paired with self-sufficient and empathetic processes. It helps the patient to determine what areas and emotional well-being need to be addressed. The counselor will work with the patient in order to help him or her to develop love and trust in the self.

61. When both substance abuse and a mental disorder are present, they are considered a:

A. Dual addictive disorder

B. Dual diagnosis

C. Double addiction

D. Double diagnosis

Answer: B. Dual diagnosis

Explanation: By implementing the proper treatment plan for co-occurring mental disorders, the process of recovery will be much easier for the individual and increase their chance for success.

62. Which configuration style is a less forceful approach to recovery, and may offer better results for some patients?

A. Gentle approach

B. Multiple intervention approach

C. Unique approach

D. Addiction approach

Answer: A. Gentle approach

Explanation: The gentle approach is a less forceful approach to recovery, which may offer better results for some patients. The multiple intervention approach uses multiple intervention techniques when the patient is reluctant to accept their mental disorder. The unique approach is used when substance abuse and a mental disorder are both present, and a unique treatment plan must be used for the patient.

63. The New Beginnings Center provides a wide range of therapy services and helps to implement the services into the patient's everyday life. This therapy includes job assistance, skills building, and other valuable resources. What type of treatment model does this rehabilitation center use?

A. Assertive Community Therapy Model

B. Broker Generalist Model

C. Process Treatment Model

D. Strategy-Based Model

Answer: A. Assertive Community Therapy Model

Explanation: Assertive community therapy provides a wide range of therapy services. The assertive community therapy model has seven areas of emphasis and creates a natural setting for client care.

64. The Primary Treatment Assessment Process involves all of these EXCEPT:

A. Detecting special skills or defects within the patient

B. Providing basic supplemental needs to the patient

C. Identifying the level of regular ability to function with the patient

D. Detecting various patient success strategies

Answer: D. Detecting various patient success strategies.

Explanation: The Primary Treatment Assessment Process focuses on addiction treatment and identification of various patient needs for common services. This is done during the assessment process and involves detecting special skills or defects en within the patient, providing basic supplemental needs, identifying the level of regular ability to function, and detecting various patient risk strategies.

65. Decisions made by a counselor in a manner that regards the patient's best interest are considered:

A. Ethics decisions

B. Moral decisions

C. Truthful decisions

D. Professional decisions

Answer: B. Moral decisions

Explanation: Moral decisions are decisions made by a counselor in a manner that regards the patient's best interest. The decision that is made involves policy, the right attitude, and appropriate behaviors on a case-by-case basis.

66. A set of principles that create moral decisions involving patient care and value are:

A. Moral principles

B. Rules and regulation principles

C. Ethical principles

D. Law principles

Answer: C. Ethical principles

Explanation: Ethical principles create moral decisions involving patient care and value. Aspects of ethical practice include moral decisions, laws, and principles.

67. What does a patient have to sign in order to share confidential counseling records with another mental health facility?

A. A disclosure of ethics

B. A disclosure of records

C. A prior authorization

D. An information authorization

Answer: B. A disclosure of records

Explanation: In order for the information to be provided to the medical professional, there must be a prior authorization provided by the patient. Authorization is made when the patient signs a disclosure of records, which is done in the presence of the counselor who is providing the treatment to the patient. With the area of confidentiality regarding ethics, a judgment of overall privilege for proper administration of justice allows information given under certain exceptions.

68. A process where a counselor needs to take steps in order to determine whether serious danger is present is called:

A. Duty to warn

B. Duty to disclose

C. Authorization to warn

D. Authorization to disclose

Answer: A. Duty to warn

Explanation: Duty to warn is a process where the counselor providing treatment to the patient needs to determine whether serious danger is present. To assess the situation, the counselor should first talk to the supervisor in charge of the treatment plan to obtain assistance in making the correct decision. After this, the case should be referred to the police, so the potential victim can receive the care that he or she needs in order to reduce serious harm.

69. What aspect of pharmacology determines the level of addiction in a person?

A. The strength of the drug

B. The person's gender

C. The method of administration

D. All of the above

Answer: D. All of the above

Explanation: Gender, method of administration, and strength of the drug all determine the level of addiction present.

70. A substance prescribed to a patient to treat a condition, which may have a potential for abuse, is called:

A. A substance

B. A drug

C. A medicine

D. All of the above

Answer: C. A medicine

Explanation: A drug is an illegal substance used to create a high within the body. A medicine is a substance prescribed to a patient to treat a condition. It may have a potential for abuse, and if this is present, the use of the drug should be monitored.

71. A state that occurs when drug or alcohol abuse has occurred for a prolonged period of time is:

A. Misuse

B. Dependence

C. Psychological dependence

D. Reverse dependence

Answer: B. Dependence

Explanation: Dependence is a state that occurs when drug or alcohol abuse has occurred for a prolonged period of time. The person can become both mentally and physically addicted to the drug. Misuse is using a drug in a manner, or for a reason, that differs from how it was prescribed. This type of use is unintentional. Psychological dependence occurs when a person has a strong mental urge to use a drug to experience the effects considered to be pleasant (drug or alcohol used to reach a euphoric state of mind).

72. When a person uses another drug form to lessen the withdrawal they are experiencing from their drug of choice, it is called:

A. Dependence

B. Abuse

C. Cross-dependence

D. Reverse dependence

Answer: C. Cross-dependence

Explanation: With cross-dependence, a person may use another drug form to lessen the withdrawal they are experiencing from their drug of choice. Abuse is using a drug in a manner other than that prescribed, with the intention of getting high, such as taking too much of one drug within a short period of time.

73. This causes a person to become more sensitive to a drug over a period of time, rather than less sensitive:

A. Tolerance

B. Reverse tolerance

C. Psychological dependence

D. Physical dependence

Answer: B. Reverse tolerance

Explanation: Reverse tolerance will cause a substance to have a higher level of impact on a person when taken.

74. The amount of drug needed by the person in order for it to be effective is called:

A. The lethal dose

B. The half-life dose

C. The therapeutic dose

D. The maximum dose

Answer: C. The therapeutic dose

Explanation: The therapeutic dose is the amount of drug needed by the person in order for it to be effective.

75. What type of risk exists with intravenous drug use?

A. The risk of infection

B. The risk of overdose

C. The risk of addiction

D. All of the above

Answer: D. All of the above

Explanation: When drugs are taken through injections, there are additional risks that are present. While the risk of overdose is high with this method of administration, the risk of contracting a disease is also increased greatly. This is because if a needle is shared, disease can be easily spread.

76. What is the street name for a fungal substance that grows naturally in certain regions of the world and gives euphoria when eaten?

A. "Shrooms"

B. "Acid"

C. "Buttons"

D. "DMT"

Answer: A. "Shrooms"

Explanation: "Shrooms" or "magic mushrooms" contain a psychedelic/euphoric substance called psilocybin.

77. When a urine drug test is sent to the laboratory, this can:

A. Provide faster results

B. Provide sterile results

C. Provide more accurate results

D. All of the above

Answer: C. Provide more accurate results

Explanation: If the test needs additional screening, it can be sent to a laboratory, which will provide more accurate testing results. This includes the amount of the drug present in the urine, which can indicate the amount being used and the last time the drug was used.

78. How is saliva testing done?

A. The patient spits some saliva in a cup, which is sent to the laboratory.

B. The patient coughs up some saliva, and puts into a test tube.

C. A swab made from cotton material is used to take a sample of the saliva on the inside of the cheek, and then the swab is enclosed in a sterilized container that will be sent to a lab for testing.

D. A syringe made from plastic used to take a sample of the saliva on the inside of the cheek, and then the syringe is enclosed in a sterilized container that will be sent to a lab for testing.

Answer: C. A swab made from cotton material is used to take a sample of the saliva on the inside of the cheek, and then the swab is enclosed in a sterilized container that will be sent to a lab for testing.

Explanation: The mucus membranes within the mouth will have traces of the drug, which will then move into the saliva. This testing is done by using the swab on the inside of the cheek, and then enclosing the swab in a sterilized container that will be sent to a lab for testing.

79. Regardless of the amount or number of drugs being assessed, when conducting blood toxicology testing, how many samples or vials are required?

A. 1

B. 2

C. 3

D. 4

Answer: A. 1

Explanation: One blood sample is all that is needed, regardless of the amount of drugs being assessed.

80. If a person has many fights and altercations, and eventually suffers from a car accident, this is a sign of:

A. Impairment due to substance use

B. Casual use of a substance

C. Normal behavior for a young person

D. None of the above

Answer: A. Impairment due to substance use

Explanation: Impairment causes the inability to keep a job or attend school, use of substances in high risk situations, such as while driving, legal consequences due to the use of drugs, and encountering conflicts due to alcohol or substance use.

81. Who would have a lower tolerance to alcohol?

A. A 155-pound woman

B. A 275-pound man

C. A 125-pound man

D. A 132-pound woman

Answer: D. A 132-pound woman

Explanation: Similar to the reaction that some people have to certain foods, some people may be unable to tolerate alcohol, even when consumed in small amounts. Their bodies will act adversely to the substance, and behavioral issues will occur. Women tend to have a lower tolerance to alcohol then men.

82. Signs of genetic factors associated with addiction in a young person include all of the following EXCEPT:

A. Bubbly personality

B. Lack of social skills

C. Violent behaviors

D. Impulsive behaviors

Answer: A. Bubbly personality

Explanation: When addiction occurs based on genetic factors, signs of addiction often show before the substance is used. Signs are seen at a young age, which include violent behaviors, impulsive behaviors, and lacking social skills.

83. When providing counseling and treatment for a recovering addict, the counselor should provide several levels of care. Which of the following would NOT be an appropriate type of therapy?

A. Family therapy

B. Group therapy

C. Individual therapy

D. Cultural therapy

Answer: D. Cultural therapy

Explanation: The counselor should provide several levels of patient care to the patient, and individual, group, and family therapy should be used in conjunction when appropriate.

84. For those going through recovery, the concept of recovery in addiction is a plan that works by implementing a treatment program that provides:

A. Transformational change

B. Temporary change

C. Immediate change

D. Permanent change

Answer: A. Transformational change

Explanation: The concept of recovery in addiction is a plan that works by implementing a treatment program that provides transformational change in those who are going through the process of recovery. As knowledge continues to expand, the methods used to treat addiction also expand and various techniques used together can provide recovery to patients.

85. The chance of a successful recovery from addiction is increased when:

A. Therapy is used to help the patient gain new skills.

B. The patient's mental health issue is treated.

C. The patient's physical health issue is treated.

D. Genetic factors are addressed.

Answer: B. The patient's mental health issue is treated.

Explanation: By treating the patient's mental health issue, the chance of a successful recovery is increased. Therapy is used to help the patient gain the skills needed for long-term recovery.

86. A group of individuals are working together in order to provide education on drug use to a group of young African American adolescents. What is this group called?

A. A prevention group

B. A treatment group

C. A rehab group

D. An intervention group

Answer: A. A prevention group

Explanation: Prevention groups are defined as a group of individuals who are working together in order to provide education on drug use to a target group. The groups included in the process of intervention include the general population, at-risk individuals, and high-risk individuals.

87. The main goal of a prevention group is:

A. To offer treatment to at-risk youths

B. To offer a safe house to at-risk youths

C. To stop drug use from occurring

D. To stop the transmission of HIV

Answer: C. To stop drug use from occurring.

Explanation: The main goal of a prevention group is to stop drug use from occurring, but also to address the issue of abuse if it should occur by catching it while in the early stages.

88. A group of individuals reduces the amount of demand present for drugs and alcohol by providing those in the community with appropriate treatment methods. This is an example of:

A. Rehabilitation

B. Prevention

C. Treatment

D. Community service

Answer: B. Prevention

Explanation: Preventive methods include reducing the available supply of drugs and alcohol through appropriate measures, including legal assistance, reducing the amount of demand present for drugs and alcohol by providing those in the community with appropriate treatment methods, and continuing development of treatment centers to improve the level of care offered.

89. A youth organization is promoting safe alternatives by offering community activities to schoolchildren and providing education regarding the dangers associated with drug and alcohol use. This is an example of:

A. Primary prevention

B. Secondary prevention

C. Tertiary prevention

D. Quaternary prevention

Answer: A. Primary prevention

Explanation: Primary prevention is used for young people or those with little to no history of drug/alcohol abuse. It is applied by promoting abstinence from drugs and alcohol, teaching refusal skills to those who haven't used it, increasing usage policies, such as the age limit to buy alcohol, providing education on the dangers associated with drugs and alcohol use, and promoting safe alternatives by offering community activities to younger people.

90. The term "referral" means:

A. Meeting other counselors for discussions regarding patients

B. Assisting a patient with using support services and available resources

C. Providing alcohol and drug education to patients

D. Attending an NA, AA, or Al-Anon meeting with the patient

Answer: B. Assisting a patient with using support services and available resources.

Explanation: If a patient requires addiction support that does not fall within the scope of your facility, you may need to refer him or her. A referral involves assisting the patient to use support services and available resources.

91. What is the counselor most concerned with during a crisis interview with a patient?

A. Getting all the pertinent information possible

B. What the immediate response should be

C. The patient's family dynamics and available support systems

D. Focusing questions on the present situation and the patient's coping skills

Answer: A. Getting all the pertinent information possible

Explanation: During a crisis interview, it is important to gather all pertinent information that you possibly can. This will allow you to make decisions regarding the patient's care and determine what needs to be done.

92. A single mother with four children comes into the clinic where you work. When discussing her current drug use, she tells you she has not been back to the apartment for three days, but left her 10-year-old son in charge. What should you do?

A. Admit her for immediate treatment and arrange for childcare.

B. Contact child protective services to report this.

C. Call law enforcement to have her arrested for child neglect.

D. Send her home to make arrangements for childcare before returning for treatment.

Answer: B. Contact child protective services to report this.

Explanation: Because the mother left the children alone, they are at risk for harm and neglect has occurred. The proper authorities should be notified, as the children may need medical care and other services.

93. A patient is showing signs of denial due to discrepancies he makes during the intake interview. Which one of the following statements should the counselor make that would be MOST appropriate?

A. "You have told me several different things. Which one is the truth?"

B. "I am not sure I understand you, so please clarify this."

C. "Denial is part of addiction."

D. "Your story is quite confusing."

Answer: D. "Your story is quite confusing."

Explanation: To let the patient know that you are aware of the discrepancies, the counselor should inform him of this.

94. One tertiary prevention measure a treatment center could use is:

A. Using pharmaceutical approaches

B. Admitting the patient to a homeless shelter

C. Exposing the addict to triggers

D. Educating the patient on prevention of STDs

Answer: A. Using pharmaceutical approaches.

Explanation: Tertiary prevention is used when drug or alcohol use and abuse has become progressive. The counselor must apply intervention processes to stop drug use and encourage recovery, send the patient to an appropriate detoxification (detox) facility, use recovery treatment centers after detox is complete, use a specialized approach to treatment which includes desensitizing users to triggers, and using pharmaceutical approaches to help the recovery process.

95. The intervention process is successful when applied using the correct measures of:

A. Attached caring

B. Detached caring

C. Recovery

D. Healing

Answer: B. Detached caring

Explanation: The intervention process involves meeting with the family and significant others of the addict, who will be assisted through the process with the help of a counselor. The process is successful when applied using the correct measures of detached caring.

96. One of the benefits of intervention is that it stops denial of the addiction in:

A. The addict

B. The family members

C. Significant others

D. All of the above

Answer: D. All of the above

Explanation: While an intervention is not always successful for the addict, the process can still be successful for those involved. This is because it offers different benefits, which include coming together for the first time as a family since the addiction, started, learning techniques that each family member can use for their own self-help process, stopping denial of the addiction in both family members and the addict, and learning as a group how to stop enabling addiction.

97. A person who uses drugs often and has had a few issues occur as a result of the use is considered a/an:

A. Heavy and non-problematic user

B. Heavy user with serious problems

C. Heavy user with moderate problems

D. Moderate and non-problematic user

Answer: C. Heavy user with moderate problems

Explanation: A non-user is a person that does not or has not used substances. A moderate and non-problematic user uses some substances occasionally, but the use has not had a negative effect on the patient's life so far. A heavy and non-problematic user uses substances heavily, but hasn't had negative effects occur in health or life. A heavy with serious problems uses substances very often, and has had many negative events occur due to use. A heavy with moderate problems uses often and has had a few issues occur as a result of the use.

98. This person is unable to stop drugs due to physical and mental addiction. Also, the use and abuse of substances has caused issues in the patient's personal life, as well has had a negative effect on their health:

A. Heavy user with serious problems

B. Heavy user with moderate problems

C. Dependent and addicted with life and health problems

D. Dependent and addicted with health problems

Answer: C. Dependent and addicted with life and health problems

Explanation: Dependent and addicted with life and health problems describes a person who is unable to stop drugs due to physical and mental addiction, and who has issues in their personal life, as well as negative effects on their health.

99. During this treatment step, the counselor helps the addict stop use of the drug through detox and the use of pharmaceutical alternatives:

A. Step 1 - Identify

B. Step 2 - Assessment

C. Step 3 - Stabilize

D. Step 4 - Rehabilitate

Answer: C. Step 3 - Stabilize

Explanation: During the third step (stabilization), the counselor helps the addict stop addiction to the substance using appropriate methods. Some methods include detox and use of pharmaceutical alternatives in order to help stop mental addiction to drugs, and creating a secure recovery foundation.

100. The counselor determines the proper long-term treatment program for the patient based upon the issues detected during the assessment and development of overall treatment plan. What treatment step is this?

A. Step 1 - Identify

B. Step 2 - Assessment

C. Step 3 - Stabilize

D. Step 4 - Rehabilitate

Answer: D. Step 4 - Rehabilitate

Explanation: To rehabilitate the addict, the counselor determines the proper long-term treatment program for the patient based upon the issues detected during the assessment and development of overall treatment plan.

101. Rehab centers that offer the same type of care as inpatient rehabilitation facilities, except the patient leaves the facility and goes home after the treatment is completed each day, are called:

A. Co-occurring treatment centers

B. Day treatment centers

C. Aftercare treatment centers

D. Outpatient treatment centers

Answer: D. Outpatient treatment centers

Explanation: Inpatient facilities are designed to treat patients who stay at the facility over the entire course of treatment. Treatment generally lasts from one to six months. Outpatient facilities offer the same type of care as inpatient rehabilitation facilities, except the patient leaves the facility and goes home after treatment is completed each day.

102. Of the following statements about goal setting for the treatment of addiction, which is NOT true?

A. Goal setting is an important part of the treatment program

B. Goals are based on the counselor's desires

C. Goals are based on the patient's desires

D. Goals are created using realistic measures

Answer: B. Goals are based on the counselor's desires

Explanation: An important part of any treatment program is to set goals with the patient. Goals are based upon the patient's desires, and are created using realistic measures.

103. Which of the following is NOT a benefit of goal setting for the recovering addict:

A. Makes is easier for the patient to achieve sobriety

B. The patient reviews goals regularly to keep perspective

C. Helps the patient stay on track

D. Gives the patient success stories to share with others

Answer: A. Makes is easier for the patient to achieve sobriety

Explanation: When goal setting is used, it offers several benefits, but achieving sobriety will never be easy for a patient.

104. This type of therapy gives the patient the opportunity to relate to others who are going through similar issues:

A. Individual therapy

B. Couples therapy

C. Group therapy

D. Family therapy

Answer: C. Group Therapy

Group therapy offers the patient the ability to participate in a group setting with peers who also face addiction. Group therapy gives the patient the opportunity to relate to others who are going through similar issues, as well as to develop a support team.

105. The 12-step approach was created as the original principle for:

A. Alcoholics Anonymous

B. Group therapy

C. Individual counseling

D. Family therapy

Answer: A. Alcoholics Anonymous

Explanation: Many self-help groups use the 12 steps, which were created as the original principles for Alcoholics Anonymous.

106. "Made a searching and fearless moral inventory of ourselves." Which of the 12 steps is this?

A. Step

B. Step 3

C. Step 4

D. Step 5

Answer: C. Step 4

Explanation: Step 4. "Made a searching and fearless moral inventory of ourselves."

107. "Were entirely ready to have God remove all these defects of character." Which of the 12 steps is this?

A. Step 6

B. Step 7

C. Step 8

D. Step 9

Answer: A. Step 6

Explanation: Step 6. "Were entirely ready to have God remove all these defects of character."

108. "Continued to take personal inventory and when we were wrong promptly admitted it." Which of the 12 steps is this?

A. Step 9

B. Step 10

C. Step 11

D. Step 12

Answer: Step 10

Explanation: Step 10. "Continued to take personal inventory and when we were wrong promptly admitted it."

109. Who regulates the universal precautions and guidelines?

A. Occupational Safety and Health Administration (OSHA)

B. Centers for Disease Control and Prevention (CDC)

C. American Medical Association (AMA)

D. American Drug Council (ADC)

Answer: A. Occupational Safety and Health Administration (OSHA)

Explanation: All addicts should be considered to be infected with HIV, whether test results confirm this or not. The universal guidelines fall under the national Institute of Occupational Safety and Health Administration (OSHA).

110. HIV is a virus that is contagious and can be spread via:

A. Urine

B. Physical contact

C. Airborne transmission

D. Blood and body fluids

Answer: D. Blood and body fluids

Explanation: HIV is a virus that is contagious and can be spread from one person to another via blood and body fluids. HIV is a growing epidemic among IV drug users.

111. This disease has the fastest transition rate among all STDs:

A. Hepatitis B Virus (HBV)

B. Hepatitis A Virus (HAV)

C. Human Immunodeficiency Virus (HIV)

D. Influenza Virus

Answer: C. Human Immunodeficiency Virus (HIV)

Explanation: Studies show that the HIV has the fastest transition rate among all other sexually transmitted diseases (STDs).

112. One way HIV is transmitted in social groups is:

A. When group members share eating utensils

B. When members engage in unprotected sexual activity with multiple other members of the group

C. When group members share sleeping bags and bed linens

D. All of the above

Answer: B. When members engage in unprotected sexual activity with multiple other members of the group

Explanation: If members of a group have regular unprotected sex with multiple members, they risk transmitting HIV and other STDs.

113. What happens when the HIV virus is exposed to air?

A. It will die

B. It lives for five minutes and then will die

C. It lives for ten minutes and then will die

D. It lives for 30 minutes and then will die

Answer: A. It will die.

Explanation: The HIV virus lives within cells and dies once it is outside of the body.

114. HIV transmission is more likely when:

A. The person is younger than 16 years.

B. The person is a female.

C. The person has a suppressed immune system.

D. The person has an active immune system.

Answer: C. The person has a suppressed immune system.

Explanation: Once the HIV virus is passed to another individual, it spreads rapidly. The virus begins within the area that it entered, typically the blood or sexual organs. It will then quickly spread and start attacking the body.

115. What is the purpose of providing treatment for someone who has HIV in the early stages?

A. It can be cured.

B. The process of infecting the entire body can be delayed.

C. The virus can be suppressed for 2 years.

D. There is no reason to give treatment in the early stages.

Answer: B. The process of infecting the entire body can be delayed.

Explanation: Treatment can be provided for HIV when it is in its earliest stages. While there is no cure for this type of disease, when you provide treatment for those who are in early stages of the disease, the actual process of infecting the entire body can be delayed.

116. Of the following symptoms, which is NOT one that is related to HIV?

A. Lesions

B. Fevers

C. Fatigue

D. Hearing loss

Answer: D. Hearing loss

Explanation: Early symptoms of HIV include dark lesions occurring on the body, changes in vision, fatigue, and unexplained fevers.

117. Why is sexual intercourse such a risky behavior for women who have drug addictions?

A. Sex is often offered to men in exchange for drugs when addiction has progressed

B. Sex is often part of the drug scene

C. Oral sex can lead to herpes

D. All of the above

Answer: A. Sex is often offered to men in exchange for drugs when addiction has progressed.

Explanation: As HIV and other STDs are more prevalent among other drug users, when a female addict turns to offering sex to men in exchange for drugs, she puts herself at greater risk to contract an infection.

118. The process of risk reduction counseling involves using substance-abuse prevention in order to:

A. Educate addicts on problems with addiction

B. Stop the spread of STDs

C. Stop the spread of pneumonia

D. Offer counseling sessions

Answer: B. Stop the spread of STDs.

Explanation: The process of risk reduction counseling involves using substance-abuse prevention in order to stop the spread of STDs. This form of counseling offers information regarding transmission and risky behaviors.

119. How can a counselor help the addict when he or she is actively using drugs intravenously?

A. Discuss self-exams to detect issues regarding health

B. Give information on changes that help build the immune system

C. Provide the patient with information on the steps he or she needs to take for a rapid and healthy lifestyle changes

D. All of the above

Answer: All of the above

Explanation: When the addict is actively using drugs, the counselor can provide proper coping skills, give information on additional changes designed to build the immune system, discuss the benefits of exercise, teach self-exams to detect issues regarding health, and provide the patient with information on the steps he or she can take for a rapid and healthy lifestyle change.

120. The counselor can offer external resources to the recovering addict. Which of the following is NOT considered appropriate?

A. Housesitting

B. Home healthcare

C. Support groups

D. Women's groups

Answer: D Women's groups

Explanation: External resources include housesitting, a residential program, home healthcare, support groups, and info and treatment options that are available.

121. The counselor is working with a recovering addict who is HIV positive. He tells the patient there is hope for a successful recovery. The counselor wants to instill hope for the patient because when a patient feels that there is no hope for their future, it can cause:

A. Major depression

B. Anxiety

C. Serious physical illness

D. Relapse

Answer: D. Relapse

Explanation: The counselor should discuss different treatment options that are available for the patient regarding the disease. While treatment must be focused upon recovery from substance abuse, it should also be used to discuss the virus or other STD in a manner that gives hope to the patient.

122. Caseworkers and counselors should give pre-infection advice when dealing with addicts and persons in recovery. These professionals should ensure that the treatment is one aimed towards:

A. Recovery from drugs and alcohol

B. Prevention of STDs

C. Both recovery from drug and alcohol use and prevention of STDs

D. Proper education regarding well-being

Answer: C. Both recovery from drug and alcohol use and prevention of STDs

Explanation: Pre-infection advice includes proper education on the different types of STDs, how they affect a person's life, instruction on the use of standard precautions as a part of everyday life, aiming treatment towards both recovery from drugs and alcohol and prevention of STDs and taking steps to identify and stop relapse.

123. User training, knowledge, and skills regarding STDs help with educating the recovering addict regarding the transmission of STDs. To apply this in a group setting, or in a one-on-one setting, the counselor will need to:

A. Follow the instruction manual

B. Gain experience

C. Train in a classroom setting

D. Train alongside experienced mentors

Answer: D. Train alongside experienced mentors

Explanation: In some cases, counselors train alongside experienced mentors and work to apply the mental text to settings in order to gain experience.

124. The counselor uses a therapeutic technique to connect with the patient so that he does not feel alone. What is this called?

A. Creating hope

B. Altruism

C. Bonding

D. Education

Answer: C. Bonding

Explanation: The therapeutic techniques the counselor offers to patients must help them stay in recovery by creating hope.

125. The counselor helps a group member to listen and take part in different group activities in order to improve or reconnect with their social skills, such as taking part in role playing activities. What is this therapeutic technique?

A. Resolving conflicts

B. Initiating lost connections

C. Copying actions

D. Developing social skills

Answer: D. Developing social skills

Explanation: Resolving conflicts involves taking steps to resolve any conflicts with the people who reconnect by sitting in and offering positive monitoring. Initiating lost connections is where the counselor encourages members of group to reconnect with important people in their life who were lost due to the addiction, such as close friends and family members. Copying actions is where members will see positive behaviors among some other group members and want to copy and mimic these behaviors. Developing social skills is where the counselor helps a member to listen and take part in different group activities in order to improve or reconnect with their social skills, such as taking part in role playing activities.

126. Group members will have deep fears and hidden feelings arise during the discussions. What is this called?

A. Subconscious feelings

B. Copying actions

C. Personal development

D. Trust for others

Answer: A. Subconscious feelings

Explanation: With subconscious feelings, group members will have deep fears and hidden feelings arise during the discussions, which will allow these issues to be addressed and worked through.

127. Allowing recovering addicts to learn how to express negative feelings to others in a manner that leads to resolutions is called:

A. Developing trust for own feelings

B. Developing appropriate confrontational techniques

C. Developing trust for others

D. Developing behavior plan changes

Answer: B. Develop appropriate confrontational techniques

Explanation: Developing appropriate confrontational techniques allows recovering addicts to learn how to express negative feelings to others in a positive manner.

128. Why is it important for a recovering addict to develop a behavior plan for change?

A. By expressing emotions and seeing the same emotions within group members, the recovering addict will begin to develop a plan to change negative behavior patterns

B. By expressing anger with group members, the recovering addict will begin to recognize positive behavior patterns and develop a plan to maintain them

C. By expressing emotions, discussing them and getting positive feedback, the members will be able to recognize and trust their own feelings more

D. By discussing emotions to group members, the patient will gain trust for others

Answer: A. By expressing emotions and seeing the same emotions within group members, the recovering addict will begin to recognize negative behavior patterns in his or her life and develop a plan to change them

Explanation: Connecting with other positive members and the counselor will allow the recovering addict to develop a strong support group that can aid them through their recovery.

129. All of the following are benefits of crisis intervention and resolution EXCEPT:

A. Create a helping resolution with the patient

B. Secure a safe environment for the patient

C. Offer support to the patient's family

D. Help the patient create a plan for action during times of distress

Answer: C. Offer support to the patient's family

Explanation: The counselor should implement actions for crisis intervention and resolution, such as helping to create a resolution with the patient, securing a safe environment for the patient and other group members, determining the cause of the crisis, offering support and additional resources to the family and helping the patient create a plan for action.

130. This form of treatment can offer the recovering addict the ability to express deep issues and concerns that he or she may not feel comfortable with expressing within a group setting:

A. Psychoanalysis

B. Individual counseling

C. Hypnosis

D. Family therapy

Answer: B. Individual counseling

Explanation: Individual counseling offers the patients the ability to work on a one-on-one basis with counselor. This form of treatment can offer the recovering addict the ability to express deep issues and concerns that he or she may not feel comfortable with expressing within a group setting.

131. Which of the following occurs when individual counseling occurs along with group therapy?

A. The recovering addict will relapse

B. The recovering addict will completely recover

C. The recovering addict will have a better chance at recovery

D. None of the above

Answer: C. The recovering addict will have a better chance at recovery

Explanation: The counselor can provide the patient with a sense of security during the individual counseling, which will create an environment that is secure enough for the patient to acknowledge and address issues they may be afraid to confront. If individual counseling is used along with group therapy, the recovering addict has a greater chance of recovery.

132. The counselor repeats important information given by a patient so that he or she can hear what was said and reflect on it. What counseling technique is this?

A. Coping skills

B. Paraphrasing

C. Empathy

D. Active listening

Answer: B. Paraphrasing

Explanation: Paraphrasing gives the patient the ability to hear their own words – stated slightly differently - and evaluate them critically.

133. Taking complex issues the patient is facing and offering simple solutions that can be used to resolve the conflict is called:

A. Offering simplicity

B. Offering complexity

C. Using cues

D. Using reflection

Answer: A. Offering simplicity

Explanation: To offer simplicity, the counselor will take complex issues the patient is facing and offer simple solutions that can be used to resolve the conflict.

134. This form of treatment creates a secure and effective environment where the patient can discuss his or her issues in confidence, and the therapist can offer encouragement, support, and positive coping techniques:

A. Cognitive therapy

B. Open therapy

C. Talk therapy

D. Communication therapy

Answer: C. Talk therapy

Explanation: This form of therapy encourages the patient to express his or her feelings.

135. Individual counseling is usually:

A. Short-term

B. Long-term

C. Both A and B

D. Neither A nor B

Answer: C. Both A and B

Explanation: Individual counseling may be short- or long-term, based upon the patient's particular case.

136. Family members of a recovering addict can take part in:

A. Use and abuse of substances

B. Overuse of substances

C. Enabling the addict

D. All of the above

Answer: D. All of the above

Explanation: The recovering addict's family plays an important role in both the active addiction and recovery process. According to addiction experts, these people may take part in the use, abuse, or overuse of substances and enable the patient to further use drugs or alcohol.

137. To assist with family members of the recovering addict, the counselor can offer:

A. Coping techniques

B. Work opportunities

C. Referrals

D. Social services

Answer: A. Coping techniques

Explanation: The counselor working with family members can work to create change within the family structure, create techniques within the family that can help to reach a higher level of function, provide strength to the members of the family, and offer different coping techniques to family members during the therapy session.

138. When the counselor determines reasons for a family's dysfunction, examines problems, and figures out a solution for better family dynamics, he or she is using:

A. Joining

B. Education

C. Structured analysis

D. Alternative coping techniques

Answer: C. Structured analysis

Explanation: The recovering addict can utilize outside resources in order to continue on a successful recovery path. Alternative coping techniques are when the counselor teaches honest demonstration of feelings to family members so that they can express their emotions and determine how they can use them to solve issues.

139. The use of a methadone program is considered:

A. Drug use

B. Drug substitution

C. Drug rehabilitation

D. Relapse prevention

Answer: B. Drug substitution

Explanation: Drug substitution is the substitution of a legal drug for an illegal one to assist the patient in making positive life changes.

140. Many women who are subjected to abuse:

A. Go to a shelter to cope with the abuse.

B. Turn to friends to cope with the abuse.

C. Use drugs to cope with the abuse.

D. Use distraction to cope with the abuse.

Answer: C. Use drugs to cope with the abuse.

Explanation: Many women who are subjected to abuse seek partners who have problems with addiction. Counselors must determine the dynamics that surround the use and abuse.

141. With cases involving domestic violence, when the counselor encourages the addict to stop blaming the use of a substance for the cause of the battery, this technique is called:

A. Funneling

B. Emotional expression

C. Eliminating blame

D. Analyzing abuse

Answer: C. Eliminating blame

Explanation: Eliminating blame helps the patient to realize they are responsible for the abuse, not the substance.

142. All of the following are issues seen with children who are part of a household involving addiction EXCEPT:

A. Lack of feelings

B. Self-harm

C. Enhanced self-worth

D. Boundary issues

Answer: C. Enhanced self-worth

Explanation: Issues often seen with children who are part of a household involving addiction include lack of trust, no sense of self-worth, boundary issues, lack of feelings, impulsivity, self-harm, and other negative feelings projected on themselves or onto others.

143. When counseling an adolescent who lives with an addict, the counselor should determine how both the adolescent and the user may play a role within that addiction process. It is important to tell the adolescent:

A. That addiction is a disease

B. That he or she is not responsible for the addiction

C. That enabling is not likely to occur

D. That the situation will get better

Answer: B. That he or she is not responsible for the addiction

Explanation: The counselor should determine how both the adolescent and the user may play a role within that addiction process. It is important to tell the adolescent that he or she is not responsible for the addiction but that anyone can accidentally be an enabler.

144. Concerning family counseling, a continued denial of the addiction will lead to:

A. Short-term negative effects for the addict

B. Long-term negative effects for the addict

C. Short-term negative effects for the entire family

D. Long-term negative effects for the entire family

Answer: D. Long-term negative effects for the entire family

Explanation: A continued denial of the addiction will lead to long-term negative effects for the entire family, and this could result in death due to overdose, brought on by the family's unintentional enabling.

145. Assessment of the addict and the substance use/abuse involves the collection of data from the individual, as well as corroborative sources. This is done to:

A. Determine the extent of the addiction

B. Determine the addict's strengths

C. Formulate a plan of treatment

D. All of the above

Answer: D. All of the above

Explanation: Assessment is the collection of data from the individual and corroborative sources to determine the extent of the individual's problem and their strengths, weaknesses, and needs. This information is used to formulate the plan of treatment to include goals, methods and resources.

146. Substance abuse and associated treatment services should be:

A. Standardized

B. Mandatory

C. Regulated

D. Individualized

Answer: D. Individualized

Explanation: Substance abuse and associated treatment services should be individualized and appropriate to the needs of the patient.

147. During inpatient treatment, what should be used to ensure that the patient receives all necessary services in a timely and coordinated manner?

A. An intense plan

B. A case manager

C. An educated counselor

D. A psychologist

Answer: B. A case manager

Explanation: Case management should be used to ensure that patients receive all necessary services in a timely and coordinated manner. The utilization of individual, group, and family/significant other counseling should be utilized as needed to assist in meeting the needs of the patient.

148. Recover and relapse are:

A. Ongoing processes

B. Terminal processes

C. Short-term events

D. Intermediate events

Answer: A. Ongoing processes

Explanation: Recovery and relapse are both ongoing processes, not an event. Thus, relapse prevention should be approached as a process with the identification of individualized triggers and a plan to confront those triggers should they occur. Relapse prevention should be made a valuable part of the client's aftercare program and discharge goals.

149. Abstinence violation effect refers to:

A. What happens when a person fails to abstain from a negative habitual behavior

B. What happens when a person attempts to maintain a positive habitual behavior

C. What happens when a person fails to maintain sobriety

D. What happens when a person successfully maintains sobriety

Answer: A. What happens when a person fails to abstain from a negative habitual behavior

Explanation: AVE relates to what happens when a person fails to abstain from a negative habitual behavior, such as drug use, and then faces conflict and guilt.

150. The Type One Professional Experience Questionnaire examines:

A. Psychological and behavioral issues involved in the addiction process

B. Psychological issues involved in the addiction process

C. Spiritual issues involved in the addiction process

D. Behavioral issue involved in the addiction process

Answer: A. Psychological and behavioral issues involved in the addiction process

Explanation: The Professional Experience Questionnaire is a 40-question test that examines psychological and behavioral issues involved in the addiction process.

CPSIA information can be obtained at www.ICGtesting.com
Printed in the USA
BVOW06s1917300614

357801BV00011B/102/P